You need to learn how to walk before you can run. And repeatable, sustainable innovation only occurs when companies commit to a consistent set of methods, tools and processes. Make Us More Innovative is a refreshing primer on how to develop and execute an innovation strategy. Jeffrey Phillips offers a wealth of company examples embedded within a systematic framework for achieving growth through innovation. It doesn't matter if you hail from an established or emerging industry, this book is a must-read for anyone tasked with making their company more innovative.

—Saul Kaplan
Chief Catalyst, Business Innovation Factory

Make Us More Innovative is a valuable tool for any business hoping to understand and create a culture of innovation. Phillips does a good job of laying out all the steps that will help you make your innovation initiative a reality.

—Roger von Oech
Author of "A Whack on the Side of the Head" and the Creative Whack Pack

For those seriously interested in building a systemic innovation capability, Jeffrey Phillips takes the reader on a realistic tour of what is required for success. Make Us More Innovative provides a detailed blueprint to guide development of critical pieces in the puzzle.

—Jeneanne Rae
Co-Founder and President, Peer Insight LLC

MAKE US MORE INNOVATIVE

Make us more Innovative

Critical Factors for Innovation Success

Jeffrey Phillips

OVO Innovation

iUniverse, Inc.

New York Lincoln Shanghai

Make us more Innovative

Critical Factors for Innovation Success

iUniverse books may be ordered through booksellers or by contacting:

iUniverse
2021 Pine Lake Road, Suite 100
Lincoln, NE 68512
www.iuniverse.com
1-800-Authors (1-800-288-4677)

Because of the dynamic nature of the Internet, any Web addresses or links contained in this book may have changed since publication and may no longer be valid.

The views expressed in this work are solely those of the author and do not necessarily reflect the views of the publisher, and the publisher hereby disclaims any responsibility for them.

ISBN: 978-0-595-48425-6 (pbk)
ISBN: 978-0-595-60516-3 (ebk)

Printed in the United States of America

CONTENTS

Praise for Make us more Innovative

Make Us More Innovative is a valuable tool for any business hoping to understand and create a culture of innovation. Jeffrey Phillips does a good job of laying out all the steps that will help you make your innovation initiative a reality.

Roger von Oech
Author of "A Whack on the Side of the Head" and the Creative Whack Pack

Make us more Innovative is a process road map for successful innovation. Each step offers the innovation traveler comfort along the way. Your Mission: Use It.

Stan Gryskiewicz
Author, Positive Turbulence, and Senior Fellow, Center for Creative Leadership

Innovation doesn't begin with a great idea, it begins with this comprehensive book that takes you step by step through generating change.

Andy Cohen
Innovation Guru and Author of "Follow The Other Hand"

Make us more Innovative provides a thoughtful, step by step approach for any team seeking to improve their innovation capabilities. This is a book that will be a useful resource throughout your innovation initiative.

Joyce Wycoff
co-founder of the Innovation Network

Jeffrey's methodical approach and succinct case studies paves a path for leaders on their innovation journey, whether just starting or already underway. His writing style reminds me of thoughtful conversations we've had in the past ... practical, direct, and rich with experience and research.

Matt Calman
SVP, Process Innovation & Engineering Executive Bank of America

Innovation creates sustained profitability and growth, yet too often is seen as ad hoc and unpredictable. In *Make us more Innovative*: Critical Factors for Innovation Success, thought leader Jeffrey Phillips provides a road map for managers to create robust innovation processes that tap into the creativity in their organization to realize significant results consistently.

John Warner
Founder, InnoVenture

Jeffrey Phillips does a great job of isolating the critical success factors that can make or break your innovation efforts.

Chuck Frey
Founder and President InnovationTools.com

Jeffrey Phillips is right on the mark when he advises that companies must weave innovation throughout their organization, and innovation must be an integral part of day to day operations. *Make us more Innovative* is a practical book for working managers, with twelve concrete steps that managers can take to transform their organizations into innovative firms.

Keith Sawyer
Author of Group Genius

If *Make us more Innovative* doesn't stimulate great ideas, and galvanize innovators to push their organizations to implement more effective innovation strategies, I don't know what will. Jeffery's insights provide an excellent catalyst and roadmap to embedding innovation as a core competency in any organization.

Dan Himmerich
Principal and Chief Innovation Officer, Richworth Enterprises

As innovation moves from the edge to the mainstream, an ever increasing number of executives will find themselves in the innovation spotlight. This book will provide them the guidance and insight they need to move from fuzzy concepts of innovation, to practical, realistic steps that they can begin to undertake to move their organization forward into the future.

Jim Carroll
Futurist, Trends & Innovation Expert

Make us more Innovative provides a complete methodology for building out a strategic innovation function. It addresses critical topics ranging from strategic alignment, roles and responsibilities and cultural change to innovation process definition and portfolio management in a way that can be easily adapted and put into practice. The thinking and concepts in this book have helped us immensely throughout our formation. It's both strategic and practical—a combination rarely found together.

Chad Pomeroy
VP Innovation, WellPoint

Preface

This book is the accumulation of years of consulting experience, reading and conversations with a great number of clients and consulting colleagues. It would not be possible without the interest, encouragement and enthusiasm of some great co-workers, clients and colleagues.

I'd like to thank the folks at OVO and NetCentrics, especially Dean, Bob and Bob, who have encouraged the writing of this book and who have been very supportive of the effort. I'd like to thank a number of my colleagues in the Association for the Management of Innovation (AMI), a great group of innovators sponsored by the Center for Creative Leadership. Included in that group are Kim McEachron, Jim Mathis, Stan Gryskiewicz, Matt Calman, Val Patrick and Dan Himmerich. All read the initial drafts and provided some excellent comments and feedback.

I'd like to recognize and thank Renee Callahan for her work reading, reviewing and editing the early drafts. She asked some tough questions and made the book a better one than it might have been.

Finally, I'd like to thank my spouse, who has supported my work and been an excellent confidant and sounding board. Thanks, Catherine, for everything you've done to make this a success.

INTRODUCTION

After years of cost cutting, right sizing and outsourcing, many firms have achieved exceptional cost management and process excellence. Jack Welch transformed General Electric in the late 80s and 90s using process excellence and Six Sigma techniques, and the stock price reflected Wall Street's recognition of his work. Welch wasn't unique, however. Many other firms mimicked the GE approach and spent countless hours focused on improving internal processes, outsourcing and right sizing. While these efforts have improved bottom lines and have been rewarded by Wall Street, cost cutting and outsourcing don't impact other strategic goals like organic growth and product differentiation. While necessary, cost cutting and outsourcing will rarely create a sustainable competitive advantage. Meanwhile, over the last decade, global trade barriers have fallen and new competitors have entered the market. Competition, both on-shore and off-shore, is increasing. In the face of these new realities, firms must make determinations about their strategic direction. Given the cost advantages that many other markets (China, India, etc.) enjoy, it is unlikely that many firms can choose to compete as a low-cost provider. Few firms can survive as low cost competitors, and once that choice is made, the treadmill never stops. Rather than compete on the lowest common denominator, many firms will choose to innovate and force other competitors to react to new product and service introductions, rather than constantly seek another cost reduction.

In that instance, the question becomes: How can a firm drive new revenue growth and new profits? How can it consistently create valuable new products and services? Firms need methods to understand customer needs and create a sustained process for generating interesting new products and services to remain competitive. Innovation offers the best answer and is quickly becoming the new strategic mantra for firms of all sizes. While the need for innovation is clear, significant hurdles exist before any organization can become truly innovative. Those hurdles include strategic alignment, organizational structure, corporate culture, and many other factors. How to understand and address those significant hurdles, and implement a repeatable, sustainable innovation process, is the focus of this book.

Note the use of the phrase "repeatable, sustainable innovation process". Too many firms attempt to create panic-driven "episodic" innovation—seeking one idea they can implement quickly that will reverse the company's fortunes. If your firm is in this situation, this book is not for you.

This book is intended for individuals who have been asked to help their organizations improve their innovation capabilities. Becoming more innovative seems simple on the surface, but as you examine the tasks involved it is clear that while occasional or episodic innovation happens in many firms, few are able to sustain intentional innovation over long periods of time. The difficulties lie in the fact that for many firms, innovation is often an afterthought, a "bolt-on" team or process that does not exist within the organizational structure and is not aligned to the corporate culture, measurements or rewards. Frequently innovation initiatives are layered on top of the existing infrastructure and responsibilities, and fail to become an integral part of the day-to-day operations. Innovation becomes a life raft for firms that lack other growth options, and is often just as quickly abandoned when market conditions change. This approach is a distraction that detracts attention and credibility from the real, purposeful, intentional innovation approaches and processes that are necessary for long term innovation success.

Intentional innovation—what we call *Innovating on Purpose*™—requires a much deeper commitment to innovation as a strategic goal and objective. Repeatable, sustainable innovation occurs when there is a strategic commitment to innovation and its impacts on the organization—cultural change, changes in compensation and organizational structure, and expectations about the conversion of ideas into new products and services. Becoming a truly innovative organization is more than a facelift—it is radical surgery that can dramatically improve the life of the patient, but requires the commitment to adopt the changes necessary to implement the concepts across the organization.

Starting a new innovation initiative is a significant effort, but from our experience we can define the important phases and milestones in the journey. We've identified nine key components or factors that must be addressed as your organization matures from innovation novice to repeatable, sustainable innovation capability. These factors include items such as:

- Strategic alignment

- Innovation processes

- Clear, consistent communication

- Roles and responsibilities

The following chapters will provide an overview of each feature or component, identifying its importance and providing discrete actions your team can take. Some firms may have depth and experience in some of these components, such as cultural acceptance of innovation, or strategic alignment between the vision of the company and the capabilities of the innovators in your firm. However, few firms have deep capability in all of these important innovation components. You may need outside help—and finding the right kind of outside help is possible only if you know what you are looking for and why. It may be important for your organization to spend more time on changing the culture of the organization, rather than on strategic alignment, but all of these items should be addressed in your workplan. The order of the factors is important as well. Without strategic commitment and alignment, your innovation work faces an uphill battle.

Defining the expectations of the senior management team and aligning innovation goals with corporate goals is clearly a first priority. After that, you can begin defining innovation processes and changing the corporate culture. Moving too quickly to address items that are less important but may be easier to accomplish will simply lead to failure. Frequently we encounter innovation teams that sponsored brainstorming and idea collection without management commitment or a clear focus or outcome. These initiatives inevitably struggle. Don't think that you can shortcut one of these components—while they may not appear significant, any one of these factors can stall your initiative to the point where others will call the work into question. For example, too often our clients ask us to help them capture ideas in a consistent idea database, when they don't yet have a defined innovation team or clear processes to manage or evaluate the ideas or the capability to develop the solution or launch it in the marketplace. While it seems reasonable to start with an idea database, the processes, strategic alignment, and definition of roles and responsibilities are at least as important, and should come first. Consult the table at the end of this introduction to determine which components are most important and rank your organization to see which components are well established in your firm and which will require immediate attention.

This book was written to help the individuals who have been tasked with the responsibility to make their companies more innovative. At OVO, we specialize in helping firms implement operational plans to accomplish strategic innovation goals. In this book we do not focus on innovation "advocacy"; rather, we are interested in defining the steps necessary to build a sustainable, repeatable innovation capability and innovation culture within your organization. As much as possible, we've tried to remove the "consultant speak" and provide direct examples and actions you can take to make your innovation initiative successful as quickly as possible. Each of the innovation components we address is presented in just a few pages. Defining all the tasks necessary to complete each of these components could fill several books, so we've only provided enough information to help your team make decisions and get started. In each chapter, we've provided references to other books, authors or experts that we think can shed more light on a specific subject or topic.

This book and the concepts we present are based on our experience helping corporate teams become more innovative—and the successes and failures we've experienced. We've also been fortunate to interview and learn from other innovation consultants and to discuss the successes and failures of innovation teams from a number of Fortune 500 firms, not for profits and government agencies. To learn more about OVO and our innovation experience, please see the section at the end of the book on OVO or see our website at www.ovoinnovation.com.

Innovation requires a significant focus from your team, and a full-time commitment of people and resources. Developing an innovation approach can mean building the process while simultaneously generating and managing new ideas. In many cases you and your team won't be able to do this alone. Successfully implementing some of the key components will require skills that your innovation team does not possess, or require more time and focus than you can afford. As innovation has become more important as a strategic goal, consulting firms have grown in capability and offer a wide range of services. Understand your team's strengths and weaknesses and complement the team with appropriate consulting help.

Key innovation components

At OVO, we've identified nine components that are necessary for sustainable innovation to exist. For innovation to take root in your organization and produce results, each of these nine components must be addressed by your innovation team. In this book we'll spend a few pages addressing each component, defining its importance and the rationale for including it as an important component for innovation. In the table on the following page we introduce the components and make our recommendations for the order in which they should be addressed.

Innovation Components and Priority Order

Component	Order if possible
Aligning innovation to corporate goals	First, if at all possible; then keep under constant review
Getting the management team on board	Second
Creating an idea management process	Third
Defining the funding and approval approach	Fourth
Defining roles and allocating people	Fifth
Defining and building an innovation oriented culture	Sixth
Changing the organization chart	Seventh
Establishing innovation metrics—process and outcome	Eighth
Creating and using systems and databases	Based on participants and data volume
Opening up to ideas from other sources	Once the culture is ready
Creating an innovation portfolio	Grow over time
Innovation as an expectation	Grow over time

If you've been counting along, you've noticed that there are twelve components in the list above. The first five components are necessary to start an innovation initiative. These first five actions focus on building a platform for innovation. The next four actions become important as your firm seeks to institutionalize the innovation methodology. These actions involve cultural and organizational change to solidify the emphasis on innovation across the organization. The last three components become important as your initiative reaches maturity. These last three components are growth goals once your innovation initiative takes root and becomes sustainable.

Note that we've made specific recommendations about the order these tasks should be addressed. Establishing the commitment of the management team—

what innovation means to them, what they are willing to support and the expectations and timeframes—will dictate the scope of your innovation initiative and likely success. You may find after reviewing these actions that your firm is "mature" in some of these components, so you may be able to reorder the action list. Recognize as well that some actions—like defining an innovation process—may not take long to accomplish on paper but will take far longer than expected to implement and gain acceptance. The priority order we've suggested is important. A committed and engaged management team is critical for success, and communicating the importance of innovation will make it easier for individuals to submit ideas and encourage participation. Merely adding an idea capture system or assigning an innovation team will not be successful if the people within the organization don't understand the importance of innovation and the culture resists working with the innovation. Even if you believe your firm is experienced and has the necessary prerequisites, take a quick assessment of each of these components to ensure your work will have the buy-in necessary to gain acceptance and become sustainable. *Our experience indicates that many innovation program failures are due to a lack of corporate sponsorship, little organizational tolerance for the uncertainty and risk associated with innovation, or poor understanding of the processes and roles necessary to support sustainable innovation.* The ideas exist in most firms—what's lacking is the organizational willpower, process, and culture.

The missing piece

Finally please note that we've left out a key component of innovation in the table—the ideas. It's exceptionally rare to find a firm where there are few ideas—quite the contrary. Most senior leaders we talk with express the fact that there are plenty of ideas within their organizations. The real challenge most of these firms face is identifying the ideas that address challenges or opportunities aligned to business strategies and understanding how to evaluate and implement the best ideas. Too often, lots of ideas are generated but have little alignment to corporate strategies, and can't be implemented effectively. When this situation occurs, innovation is discredited because the effort seems to create ideas that have no value.

We advocate a "proactive" outreach to identify ideas that solve specific opportunities or challenges, but we also recognize the importance of ideas that "come over the transom". People within your business can and should provide ideas outside of scheduled ideation sessions, but those ideas must solve a specific problem or address a specific opportunity, so the ideas can be considered in context. Without context, it is difficult to understand what problem the idea solves, what opportunity the idea addresses and what value the idea may deliver.

We've found an inverse relationship between the amount of idea generation a firm needs and the cultural acceptance of innovation. Firms that have a culture that sponsors and rewards innovation find that ideas are easily generated without constant reinforcement. Conversely, in firms where cultural acceptance of innovation is lacking, idea generation is forced out in tense, artificial brainstorming efforts and then quickly ignored. So, we haven't forgotten the ideas. We are taking it as a given that most firms have some ideas floating around already. We know that the establishment of an innovation process and the encouragement of innovation within the culture will foster the creation of a lot of great ideas. For a more detailed discussion on idea generation and creativity, please see the appendix on at the end of this book.

To set the stage for your efforts, complete the simple exercise on the next page. For each of the components we've identified, please rank your organization's Readiness to adopt the concept, the Importance of the concept within your firm, the Effort necessary to implement and the Impact to the firm if that component is completed. By completing this exercise you'll identify the components that may exist in your firm and those that need to be developed. The result of this work will provide greater clarity on the initial prioritization, tasks and goals of the innovation team.

Self Assessment

Component	Readi-ness	Impor-tance	Effort	Impact
	1—low	1—low	1—low	1—low
	5—high	5—high	5—high	5—high
Alignment to strategic goals				
Getting the management team on board				
Creating an idea management process				
Defining the funding and approval approach				
Defining roles and allocating people				
Creating an innovation oriented culture				
Changing the organization chart				
Establishing innovation metrics				
Creating and using systems and databases				

How to assess the result—a representative sample

Component	Readiness	Importance	Effort	Impact
	1—low 5—high	1—low 5—high	1—low 5—high	1—low 5—high
Alignment to strategic goals	4	3	3	4
Getting the management team on board	(2)	(5)	3	5
Creating an idea management process	4	4	3	4
Defining the funding and approval approach	(2)	4	(5)	4
Defining roles and allocating people	3	3	(5)	4
Creating an innovation oriented culture	5	5	2	3
Changing the organization chart	4	3	3	(5)
Establishing innovation metrics	2	5	4	3
Creating and using systems and databases	5	3	3	4

Assessing the result:

The sample assessment on the previous page helps set the stage for an innovation initiative and identifies some areas for immediate focus. First is the importance of ensuring the buy-in of the entire management team. The assessment identifies a low state of readiness *and* a high importance of acquiring the agreement of the management team. Next, the assessment indicates low readiness in regards to funding of the team and the innovation process, and identifies a significant effort to define and create that funding. Finally, the assessment identifies a significant effort in defining and building the innovation team. In the case of this sample evaluation, these scores could reflect an organization that has a very senior champion for innovation who has not completely brought the management team on board. The assessment also reflects an organization that has had some innovation success, but in a casual, haphazard manner that downplays a formal team but recognizes the importance of a process.

Read the assessment from the top down, since the factors near the top will influence the factors further down. Identify the components that need further development (readiness) and have a high importance or high effort required to complete them. These components should attract more of your team's time and effort when building out your innovation capability plan.

Few companies will score a consistent "high" score across all of these components and attributes. What's important is to understand the strengths of the company and the gaps or areas for improvement, and to ensure a consistent implementation. For example, a firm that already has idea databases and innovation metrics in place but doesn't have innovation aligned to strategic goals has too much focus on tactical implementation and not enough on strategic alignment. A firm with that profile will struggle to raise innovation above a short term, incremental focus. As you complete this assessment, you may identify components that are relatively complete and accepted, and components that are immature or non-existent. For those immature or non-existent components, it's important to understand the role they play for sustainable innovation, and the effort necessary to address that need. For instance, a firm that has senior management commitment to innovation but has not addressed cultural change will want to work on those issues before implementing innovation metrics. These components tend to cascade in terms of influence from top to bottom. Low scores near the top of the matrix (Strategic Alignment, Committed Management Team, Defined Innovation Process) will trump higher scores lower in the matrix.

There is no magic or "right" score within the assessment. The scores for a firm focused on disruptive service innovation in a firm that has complete management commitment may be very different from a firm focused on incremental innovation in a very different industry. The assessment should be used to help you and your team take an impartial, critical look at your firm and identify the strengths of the organization and areas for improvement as you build your innovation capabilities.

How to use this book

This book is full of examples and recommended actions for a person or team getting started on an innovation initiative. We've written the book to address several audiences. Our first intended audience are the firms just beginning to create a sustainable innovation capability. If your role is to create an innovation capability from scratch, consider starting at the beginning of the book and working through each chapter in order. Start with the most strategic issues like strategic alignment and management commitment, and work your way through the process definition to developing a database of ideas. If you attack the opportunity in this way, you'll have a logical, top-down approach, which we've proven to be successful in a number of engagements. Once you've completed the first section of the book and implemented its actions and recommendations, you'll have a well organized, intentional innovation process.

The second intended audience is those firms that have started an innovation initiative but are not achieving the level or consistency of results that were expected, and those who wish to create a more consistent innovation capability across their entire organization. Individuals in the second category may find that their firm has experience in some of the components but need to improve or implement some of the recommendations. We've written this book so that each chapter can stand on its own as a guide for a specific requirement or phase of the innovation effort. For some readers, it may make more sense to pick the chapters that are most relevant for their specific needs, and use just those actions and recommendations.

For either approach, your goal as you complete the book and implement the recommendations is a consistent, defined innovation program in line with strategic goals, generating ideas that are carefully considered and nurtured through a defined innovation process in an organization that is supportive of innovation and recognizes the value innovation can provide.

Your mission, if you
choose to accept it ...

After years of cost-cutting and outsourcing, many firms have shed unproductive or unprofitable products or lines of business and returned to their core strengths. While those efforts have been wonderful for the bottom line, years of trimming and cost cutting have not done much for revenue growth, differentiation, competitive advantage, or profitability. Now that all of the non-essential functions have been stripped away, growth and differentiation are becoming important strategic initiatives. Growth comes from offering the existing products and services to new customers (marketing segmentation) or offering new products and services to existing or new customers (innovation). Given the difficulty of identifying new "Blue Oceans" where customers have extensive unmet needs, innovation holds the greatest opportunity to achieve revenue growth with new products and services, targeting your existing customers as well as attracting new customers and entering new markets. Innovation has become the corporate strategic watchword, and it's likely you've found this book because you, or someone you know, have been assigned what may seem to be the Mission Impossible: *Make us more innovative.*

On its face, creating a process and culture which supports innovation may seem daunting. By our estimation, there are nine major components required to build a successful innovation capability, and several more components to consider once the capability is mature. Unfortunately, there's really not a simple one in the list, and all of them require change. So, just as the journey of a thousand miles begins with a single step, the development of an innovation focus begins with some simple considerations—defining your tasks, role and responsibility effectively, defining innovation processes, establishing innovation teams, effectively communicating the processes and goals to others in the organization.

If we use the metaphor of a journey to provide an analogy for the innovation initiative, we can compare the decisions that you'll be making to that of a traveler coming to a fork in the road. You can't simply take just any fork in the road, however. Experienced travelers use maps and guidebooks to steer them to their destination. For innovation initiatives, however, there are few maps and often many equally valid alternatives. What's needed in many circumstances is a guidebook to help direct the innovation team to greater chances of success.

This book is meant to provide you and your team with some guidance about the decisions and prioritizations you are making right now, and to define some steps to take to simplify the decision process and get started on the innovation initiative. In other words, we'll help you choose the right forks and provide the road signs along the way.

Your innovation team is starting what can be one of the most important strategic initiatives within your company. Few initiatives have the ability to increase revenue, grow profits and increase differentiation, and impact the entire organization. While there are some significant benefits from innovation, there will be some dramatic challenges. Strategic alignment, cultural change, bureaucratic boundaries, and a host of other roadblocks await your initiative. Any one of these factors can slow or even kill an innovation initiative. After all, *your goal is not to create another "bolt-on" process, but to change the way your organization thinks about creating new products and services—and make innovation an expectation for everyone within the business.*

Don't just stand there

Probably the biggest challenge you face is just getting started—understanding all the components or facets of the opportunity and prioritizing them. The most important action to take is to bring some order to the chaos and establish plans so you can get started. Inertia is one of the most significant roadblocks to an innovation initiative, so providing a clearly defined and prioritized set of tasks will enable you to manage the process and get started. Do something—even if that something is not the "perfect" solution. Recognize that your early efforts will lead to more failure than success. Demonstrate how the learning associated with failure is incorporated into an improved process or set of expectations and recognize those who are innovating according to your plans and goals. Then, do it all again, incorporating everything you've learned and setting your sights a little higher each time.

With no further ado, we'll examine each of the nine components for a successful innovation initiative and get you on your way.

OBTAINING SPONSORSHIP
AND STRATEGIC
ALIGNMENT

Background

You've been asked to help the company become more innovative because someone in the executive management team recognizes the importance of innovation for the long term success of the company. This recognition can spring from several sources. Executive vision and fear are the two most common sources. Executive vision is what we read about on the cover of the national business magazines. Steve Jobs at Apple, Yvon Chouinard at Patagonia and Arthur Lafley at P&G are good examples of leaders who recognize the importance of innovation and promote a consistent corporate strategy of innovation. These leaders are constantly stretching the boundaries and setting goals for innovation and measuring the impact of innovation in terms of market share, revenue growth and new product introductions. At the opposite end of the spectrum, many executives turn to innovation in a reactive mode rather than a positive, proactive mode. These executives are at the end of their management rope, and believe that innovation is the only means to escape a dire fate. These executives turn to innovation in the hope that innovation can provide a quick fix for their businesses. Fortunately, most executives exist somewhere in between these two extremes—comfortable in the status quo but recognizing the need for new growth initiatives. While these executives may lack the "vision" of a Jobs or Lafley, they recognize the importance of sustained innovation to drive organic growth. In recent surveys of executives by the Boston Consulting Group, over two-thirds of the executives surveyed identify innovation as a key strategic goal.

Somewhere, however, that strategic intent gets lost or garbled. One significant obstacle to innovation in most firms is the disconnect between the executive team's words and actions. Too often, executives talk about the importance of innovation, but the funds and resources necessary to implement the vision don't materialize. There are several reasonable explanations for this disconnect between words and actions. First, innovation often takes a back seat to more urgent, pressing needs, like quarterly returns. Innovation requires a significant investment before any return is recognized, and most executives are rewarded on near term metrics like financial results. Second, the executive team recognizes the importance of innovation but does not understand how to define what "innovation" means or how to fund or to measure innovation. Third, no one is quite sure what needs to be done, or what effort or cost would be involved to make the firm more innovative, to create an infrastructure where innovation can thrive. Fourth, innovation requires a long term commitment and intense management involvement and focus. The attention span of most senior management teams is simply not consistent enough for innovation to take root and grow before management's attention is directed in other areas. For these reasons, individuals who are responsible for implementing innovation initiatives often receive mixed messages and determine that the senior management team is unwilling to provide the investment necessary for sustainable innovation to take root. Need further proof? In a Boston Consulting Group survey of senior executives conducted in 2006, the top two reasons identified for the lack of innovation in most firms were *lack of time* and *lack of management commitment*. These two responses fly in the face of the stated importance of innovation. If innovation is important, the executive team will find the time, resources and commitment necessary for innovation to take root and succeed as a strategy. Given that innovation requires significant time and effort, it is easy for an innovation initiative to fall prey to issues and needs that are "urgent" but not strategically "important". Quarterly results are a constant, urgent requirement, while innovation is important but with less tangible near-term results.

As an innovation champion, you need to understand how to translate the potential outcomes of innovation so that they are discrete, understandable and align to the executive team's goals for the organization, which will attract management attention, commitment and funding. Keeping the innovation initiatives aligned with the strategic goals and directions of the firm may seem obvious, but in many instances innovation takes on a life of its own, and fails to support or reinforce key strategic initiatives. Working with the executive team to define their vision and aligning the goals and outcomes of the innovation effort to that vision is the first key to your success.

Likewise, an innovation initiative that begins without senior management oversight, commitment and sponsorship is almost always doomed from the start, since the team will find it difficult to obtain resources. Without clear management sponsorship, the team will struggle to gain credibility, attract personnel and create change within the organization. Since innovation requires change to existing processes and requires resources and funding, it requires significant sponsorship from the most senior executives to achieve success.

Case Study

We worked with a large electronics manufacturer that has a long, successful history of incremental product innovation. While moderately successful, the firm has seen its profits erode and has taken on several acquisitions in an attempt to diversify its product line. A new CFO was hired and introduced Six Sigma and Lean concepts to the organization. The organization adopted Six Sigma sporadically, but gradually adopted much of the thinking behind Six Sigma. However, as this was happening, the firm's competitors launched several new products that dramatically changed the market. Incremental innovation clearly was not enough to compete with these new product introductions. However, the executives behind the Six Sigma initiative held sway over the strategic direction of the company, placing more emphasis on cost cutting and process excellence rather than on new product development and innovation. A new initiative was created to help the company become more innovative, but struggled to gain credibility and demonstrate results. The innovation team lacked *sponsorship and alignment* with the senior management team. It failed to reach consensus with key leaders on the importance of implementing innovation processes and encouraging the firm to become more innovative. The management team was divided in its approach, and the Six Sigma team held more power than the individuals who backed the innovation initiative. After several months of false starts, the innovation team was disbanded and the individuals distributed back to various product groups and corporate marketing. The innovation team was not able to demonstrate the importance of an investment in innovation, or to change the focus of the firm from process excellence to innovation. Given the disconnect between the stated goals of innovation and the clear emphasis on Six Sigma improvements, the innovation team could not gain enough sponsorship or credibility. The innovation team lacked executive sponsorship and alignment to the short term objectives of the executive team. Clear alignment and sponsorship is critical to the creation and evolution of the innovation team.

Importance of alignment and definitions

For the success of an innovation initiative, it is important to:

- Define what "innovation" means

- Understand the expected outcomes necessary for management support

- Establish executive sponsorship

- Communicate the value that innovation can provide.

Innovation is a very broad term, and without a common definition teams throughout the firm will determine the meaning of innovation as it pertains to them. At a Frost&Sullivan conference on innovation, a speaker asked the audience, made up of senior executives from a number of Fortune 500 firms, to submit their definitions of "innovation". There were as many definitions as attendees. Within a heterogeneous group of conference attendees, that's not a problem, but within your firm it should be easy for teams to define what innovation is and that definition should be fairly consistent throughout the organization. At OVO, we believe innovation is defined as *people putting ideas into valuable action*. This definition addresses creativity—generating ideas, as well as innovation–putting the ideas into action, and the benefit—valuable action. This definition can reflect innovation as a new product to drive new revenues, or a new service for a not for profit. Think about these questions as you begin to define what innovation can mean to your business:

- Should innovation address products, services, processes, business models or all of the above?

- Is innovation meant to be incremental—small changes to existing products and services? Or disruptive, to change an industry or create a new market? Or both?

- Is innovation meant to position the firm as a leader in the industry? Should innovation initiatives help disrupt the industry?

- What are the long-term financial goals that innovation is meant to achieve?

- Should innovation be managed at the line of business or product group level, or should it be managed as an enterprise process?

- What is the appropriate level of investment in an innovation initiative, and what are the expected results and timeframes?

While these questions seem straightforward, obtaining consensus on these questions is rarely simple. However, documenting and agreeing on these definitions will eliminate a lot of cultural and bureaucratic challenges later. Defining the scope of the innovation initiative so that everyone can understand how your innovation team should be evaluated, and in what context it will work, will simplify your efforts to get started and gain credibility quickly.

Next, as the innovation leader you need to help the management team understand how innovation can make a significant impact in the measures that matter most to them—revenue growth, profits, costs, customer satisfaction or other key performance indicators. The executive team understands that innovation has some innate value, but they don't understand how to tie that value to important metrics that the business is measured against. Only by demonstrating how innovation can "move the needle" for some of those metrics will you gain the sponsorship and resources you'll need to succeed. For example, many management teams see innovation as a way to grow revenue "organically"—that is, without acquisitions of other companies. It's important that the innovation leader determine what the management team means by innovation, how the management team intends to manage the results of the work associated with innovation, and what results they expect to see from an innovation initiative. If organic growth is important, how can innovation achieve that goal?

Creating an innovation "charter" can crystallize the thinking and strategies around your innovation initiative. Rather than accept a loosely defined innovation framework and goals, work with the management team to generate a charter that they can all agree to and support. The charter should include the investments and timeframes necessary for the team to get off the ground, the types of ideas and concepts the team should pursue, the scope of the ideas and the roles and responsibilities of the team. The charter should also indicate the measurements and metrics the team will be evaluated against and set expectations for the team's priorities.

Once the charter is complete, review the charter with the innovation sponsor to ensure he or she is still "on board" to support the innovation initiative. Once the commitment is provided by the sponsor, use the charter as an initial communication document to create awareness of the initiative and the team's role and responsibilities.

Identifying misalignment

If your innovation team is not aligned to senior management and does not have a clear definition of innovation, the initiative will struggle. Without a clearly defined innovation scope, your team will pursue a wide range of ideas, some with value to the business but many that are not aligned to the strategic direction of the business. After a few months of effort, your team will expend a lot of effort and have few results to show for that investment. If your team is not in alignment with the executive team in regards to its goals and expectations for innovation, you will quickly find yourself justifying the existence of the team, which will struggle to find a sponsor. These are some common symptoms of a team that lacks alignment and sponsorship:

- Difficulty identifying which innovations are valuable

- Difficulty understanding and documenting the role of the innovation team

- Chasing a number of ideas without a clear innovation purpose

- Working on ideas that have little value to the management team

- Difficulty gaining support and buy-in from other teams or functions

For most teams in this situation, it takes only a few months to realize that the team is quite literally spinning its wheels. Many ideas have been considered and discarded, there's no clear rationale to define the ideas that have been considered, and the team has been in place long enough that the executive team starts asking for specific results and there are few to report. If your team finds itself in this situation, revisit the purpose and objectives of your team and redefine your charter to obtain the necessary sponsorship and alignment to corporate goals.

Actions

Recognize that most management teams realize innovation is important, but have little time to spend understanding the implications of an innovation initiative. Work with the executive team to understand the corporate strategy and objectives, and align the innovation initiatives to your company's appetite or capacity to adopt those innovations. Manage upward early in the process to gain sponsorship. Create an innovation strategy that defines your expectations, goals and recommended outcomes, and communicate that strategy to the executive team to obtain approval or specific redirection. Identify early the innovation outcomes that can impact important key indicators, and establish a clear scope for your innovation initiative.

Develop an innovation strategy: Document an innovation strategy that provides some guidance and direction for the management team and makes clear recommendations. Your discussions will be more productive and your initiative will move forward more quickly if you develop the outline for the innovation initiative and meet with the executive team to confirm the vision or work with them to edit your strategy. Understand that your strategy is a "strawman" that will be changed by the management team. Meet with the senior leadership and work with them to obtain a clear definition of innovation, and understand innovation aligns to and supports the corporate strategic goals. The basis of this work should become part of your team's charter, which is documented and approved by the management team and becomes part of the communication strategy to the rest of the organization.

Timeframe:	no more than three to four weeks
Deliverable:	a five to ten page strategy document detailing how the innovation initiative will support and align to corporate strategic goals
Responsible:	Innovation leader and senior executive team

Demonstrate strategic alignment: Next, once the definitions and expectations are documented, understand how innovation aligns to existing corporate goals. Should innovation initiatives focus on ideas that support the existing products and services of the firm, or seek to create new opportunities and new markets? What ideas and initiatives are palatable to the management team, and what ideas are simply non-starters? Should your innovation effort seek to solidify and expand the existing product or service offering, or seek solutions for the "white spaces" in your business, or both? In many firms, incremental innovation becomes the responsibility of existing product or service groups, while disruptive or "white space" innovation becomes the responsibility of a central innovation team. It's important to establish early in the initiative the scope of the innovation team and what ideas should be considered and what markets, ideas or strategies should be discarded. This work will avoid a common innovation problem—the generation of a lot of ideas that the management team views as not relevant to the business.

Timeframe:	no more than three to four weeks
Deliverable:	Meeting with senior executives to ensure your innovation strategy aligns to important strategic initiatives
Responsible:	Innovation leader and senior executive

Establish an innovation charter: Create a succinct innovation charter that defines in concrete terms your team's goals, expectations and measures and publish the document as part of your communication strategy. See an example on the next pages. The charter should provide details on the team's:

- Purpose

- Mission

- Priorities

- Responsibilities

- Proposed Outcomes

- Composition

- Funding

- Scope

Innovation Charter—Example

1. OPPORTUNITY	We have an opportunity to leverage the knowledge and insights of X to generate ideas that help our company create new products, new services, new business models and create new markets. Innovation is a core competency and a critical element of generating a sustained competitive advantage in the marketplace.
2. VISION	Our innovation team will sponsor innovation throughout the organization, identifying methodologies, tools and techniques to improve our capability to identify trends, recognize new product and service opportunities and create new value for our customers and prospects. The innovation team will work with internal business units to define innovation opportunities and with the entire organization to generate and evaluate ideas, which will be provided to the appropriate business units or sponsored within the innovation team.

3. MISSION	***The Innovation Team exists to:***
	Our mission is to sponsor a culture of innovation within X, and use innovation as a driver to help business units and business functions create new products, services and business models that drive new revenue, increased margins and increased market share. We'll: • *Support* innovation throughout X by providing all parts of the organization with a consistent process and methodology for idea generation and evaluation that is based upon collaboration among broad, diverse employee groups. This includes providing supporting tools and resources (online and otherwise) to foster industry knowledge, company knowledge, understanding of previously ideated topics, and spur creativity. • *Drive* innovation in "White Spaces" by identifying potential white-space ideas and incubating them until a decision is made to implement or shelve the idea. This includes analyzing information from a broad array of sources to identify trends, problems, threats, and opportunities that exist inside or outside the company then advocating ideation around significant findings. • *Advocate* innovation throughout the organization and seek ways to make the organization more innovative. This includes researching and advocating best practices, generating ideas for novel ways to keep innovation fresh in the organization, and continually seeking ways to improve the model.

4. RESPONSIBILI-TIES	The innovation team works with any group that seeks to improve its innovative capability or solve problems or seek new approaches using innovation techniques. We'll work as innovation advocates, consultants and facilitators to sponsor ideation sessions, define innovation processes, assist with the identification and evaluation of innovative ideas. We identify and synthesize trends in the environment, new technologies and approaches from within X and from external partners. We provide a broad array of individuals who can help identify new ideas, examine new approaches and methods, suggest creative methods to solve intractable problems, and assist with the implementation of recommended solutions. We define common innovation processes and sponsor innovation tools for focused ideation and idea management, and offer these tools and processes to our customers to enable them to become more innovative. We offer consultative solutions to solve problems quickly and effectively, and provide flexible solutions to meet any innovation need.

5. GOALS	*We seek:* • Breakthrough ideas—new businesses, new products, and radically different processes that diversity the product portfolio, that generate operational or cost efficiencies or develop our internal (employee) or external value proposition. • Incremental improvements—tweaks to existing businesses, products, and processes that bring operational efficiency or cost savings, provide opportunities for increased sales, or add value to our existing internal or external value proposition. *Long-term goals include:* • Creating competitive advantages • Entering new markets • Developing new products • Infusing innovation into the organization's culture • Enabling sub-organizations to be self-innovating • Formally supporting employee's time allocation to innovative behaviors • Establishing accountability for innovating throughout the business units *Measurable goals:* • X% increase in new products or services released • X% increase in revenue from new products and services • X% increase in profit margin driven by innovation
6. PRIORITIES	Define priorities based on the strategic goals and key metrics of the business

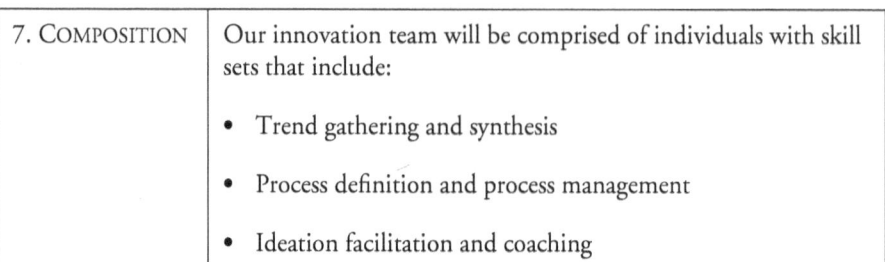

7. COMPOSITION	Our innovation team will be comprised of individuals with skill sets that include: • Trend gathering and synthesis • Process definition and process management • Ideation facilitation and coaching

The charter helps define the purpose and goals of innovation, and the responsibilities and roles of teams that are part of the innovation initiative. It also sets priorities to help determine which ideas are important and should receive further consideration, and to help the team encourage ideas or reject ideas based on the solution they provide or the opportunity they address.

The charter can easily become a communication document to share with the rest of the organization, clearly defining expectations and the roles and responsibilities of the innovation teams.

Timeframe:	One week
Deliverable:	A three to five page document that defines in explicit terms the charter, scope and responsibilities for an innovation initiative
Responsible:	Innovation leader and senior executive

Define the innovation "context": Innovation is a nebulous concept and needs more definition and context. What is necessary is to determine the scope and bounds that are acceptable within your firm for innovation (as defined by the charter) and also to determine the innovation context. What we mean by context is that most firms have a defining capability or insight that drives their value proposition. Innovation should be defined around this context. For example, W. L. Gore, a firm that many pundits identify as an innovation leader, seeks innovation around a specific technology—Teflon—and creates a wide array of products from that base technology. Apple seeks innovation around the packaging, design and user experience of consumer electronics. What is the "context" for innovation in your firm?

Establish realistic expectations: Defining and implementing an innovation initiative is challenging and time-consuming in any circumstances. Senior managers understand that the initiative will require some time for development, but will expect results far more quickly than your team is likely to be able to achieve. Set an expectation of 8 to 12 months to define, staff and deploy an innovation process, with the expectation that ideas generated early in the process won't become new products and services for possibly another year in most industries— depending on product life cycles and funding. As one senior executive we spoke with said "time is a bigger challenge than investment". Everyone is under enormous pressure to achieve quarterly goals and meet Wall Street expectations. Innovation initiatives can take a long time to develop and deploy. As an innovation leader, you must set appropriate expectations with the senior executives and the rest of the business. It can take two or three quarters to get the buy-in necessary to start an innovation initiative and begin defining an innovation process. Once the process is working effectively and ideas are flowing, it will take another three to six quarters to several years to move an idea from concept to new product or service, depending on the firm and its industry. If you fail to set appropriate expectations about the timeframes and commitments early on, your team will face repeated calls for new ideas and new products before it has had a chance to get off the ground, and will be judged a failure before it has even started.

Timeframe:	From the start of the initiative and throughout the life of the initiative.
Deliverable:	Consistent communications to set reasonable expectations
Responsible:	Innovation leader and senior executive

Identify an executive sponsor: Building an innovation capability requires significant organization change, a long term commitment, funding and resources. Many firms will pay lip service to the importance of innovation, but will not adequately support an innovation initiative. For innovation to succeed, your initiative needs a committed executive sponsor who will champion your approach to other senior executives and the organization as a whole. Without an executive sponsor, your team will not be able to receive the funding, resources or commitment from the rest of the organization. Identify a senior executive who is willing to provide the guidance and leadership necessary to develop the firm's innovation capabilities. This executive does not have to be a "C" level officer, but does need access to the "C" level executives for appropriate funding and management buy-in. Identifying and supporting the sponsor will be critical to your success, and you'll need to collaborate with your sponsor to determine the amount of risk he or she is willing to bear, and how to achieve the kinds of wins and successes that allow the sponsor to take even greater risks to support your initiative.

Timeframe:	As soon as possible
Deliverable:	A senior executive who is willing to sponsor the innovation initiative
Responsible:	Innovation leader and senior executive

More Reading/Resources

Robert Tucker has a great book about innovation titled *Driving Growth through Innovation*. In the book there is a good chapter entitled "Leading Innovation" which covers some of the same concepts as this chapter.

Erich Joachimsthaler's book *Hidden in Plain Sight* identifies a strategic approach he calls demand first innovation. In this book he details an approach for organizing the innovation strategy.

James Andrew and Harold Sirkin's book *Payback* has an excellent section on alignment and leadership and the importance of active, engaged senior management.

Additionally, Andrew and his team at Boston Consulting Group do a great job assessing the state of the market for innovation, and a consistent finding is that top executives must be active sponsors for innovation to succeed. See the August 2007 survey of senior executives at:

http://www.bcg.com/publications/files/Innovation_Aug_2007.pdf

GETTING THE
MANAGEMENT TEAM ON
BOARD

Background

Obtaining a common understanding of the goals and definitions of innovation is just the first step toward innovation success. You must now determine how to convince the entire management team to be supportive of an innovation initiative. Getting the entire management team on board is a critical and somewhat daunting task, since there are many different viewpoints and agendas at work. There are several cultural and bureaucratic pitfalls you must avoid. First, some leaders will think innovation should lie solely within their line of business or function. These individuals may harbor concerns about a general innovation initiative or seek to discourage the creation of an innovation team, claiming that their teams already "own" innovation. In fact it is often easy to find several functions or organizations within a company that claim to "own" innovation, including product development, product management, marketing, and research and development, to name just a few. The goal of your innovation initiative is not to eliminate innovation in these various locations, but to provide a more consistent set of methods, tools and processes for the organization. Second, innovation will require close working relationships across functional and geographic borders, and may require new business processes. This means encouraging teams, business functions or even lines of business to work together across organizational lines, which may conflict with existing work structures, processes, compensation schemes and corporate culture. Third, an innovation team usually begins life as a very small team that seeks to leverage resources from other teams. Innovation teams often beg, borrow, or steal personnel from other working groups until the innovation effort proves it needs full-time staff. You will need to convince managers with tight headcounts that your innovation initiative is valuable and has benefits for their organization, and that it is in their interest to provide individuals or resources to help get the initiative off the ground. So, you start your initiative with a few significant challenges—political and cultural barriers, process and organizational barriers, and limited funding and resources. How can you overcome these potential pitfalls and get started quickly?

As we identified in the first chapter, having a clear definition for innovation and an executive sponsor who can help you bring the rest of the organization on board will help tremendously. If you don't have a sponsor or a clear innovation charter, you will struggle to gain acceptance for your vision for innovation across the organization.

Case Study

In many firms, one group feels strong ownership or responsibility for innovation. In the pharmaceutical industry and other industries with a strong research and development presence, innovation is often associated with R&D. These teams often believe that they "own" innovation, and will fight to keep control of funding and ideas. In several research intensive firms we've worked in, it has become important to convince R&D or product management that while their work is important, innovation happens in other areas outside the research lab. In these firms, we've identified opportunities for innovation in marketing, sales, packaging, and services—which are clearly not the responsibility of the R&D team. As other, non-product related opportunities for innovation are identified, it becomes easier for the R&D team to acknowledge that innovation will happen in other functions in the business. Once the possibilities for innovation are identified in other, non R&D related areas, it becomes easier to create a central innovation capability and allocate tasks to teams outside of R&D without threatening the existing innovation process. Unless the management team recognizes that innovation is a shared responsibility, some business functions may undercut innovation teams to defend turf and investments. Achieving consensus within the management team requires a common definition for innovation—which we discussed in the first section—and the ability to communicate the goals and strategies of the innovation initiative.

Agreement is important

The rationale for aligning your innovation strategy to corporate goals and strategies and ensuring a consistent definition of innovation should be evident now. An innovation initiative will impact a number of business functions, product groups, and lines of business, and you'll need the support of the senior leadership team to get started and convince other management team members to come aboard. Clear, consistent communication from the executive team about the scope, role, importance, and inevitability of an innovation initiative is important, especially as the scope of the innovation team spans more than one business unit or process.

The innovation head must work with senior management to create a consistent stream of communication within the organization about the importance of innovation and the commitment of the management team. In the first chapter we noted the importance of an innovation sponsor. This communication can flow from the sponsor or another senior executive. Once the definitions and goals are established for innovation, the executive team needs to speak with one voice about the importance of innovation and the best methods to improve the innovation capability of the firm, not just to improve innovation capabilities where they may already exist. This means the head of innovation should recruit an internal communications resource to assist in developing the messages and presentations that the management team provides internally and externally to ensure the management team stays on message. In addition, the innovation leader needs to identify the formal and informal management structures to ensure all the key power brokers have been included.

Recognizing alignment problems

If the management team is not committed to the same goals for innovation, or if one team believes it "owns" innovation, challenges to your initiative will arise quickly, especially if your innovation scope is broad. Teams that feel threatened or believe they own innovation will demand participation, object to funding and claim ownership of many of the ideas your team attempts to work on. Whether these actions are subtle or overt, as the innovation team leader you'll need to react and bring the management team together to agree on basic principles or your innovation team will fail, since the existing team is already in place and has cultural acceptance and awareness. Concurrent, competing innovation initiatives will be another indication that your innovation initiative has not yet achieved corporate management alignment. If there remain a number of innovation initiatives that are not aligned to your vision or approach or duplicate existing projects, senior leadership has not yet coalesced around the value of a common innovation vision or process. Defining the scope of the existing innovation teams and the responsibilities of a new innovation initiative can go a long way to achieving buy-in from all the executive team members.

Actions

Communication is the key ingredient to help stave off infighting and struggles with existing teams that may feel threatened by a new innovation initiative. A management team that speaks consistently with one voice about innovation, its scope, and its importance, will remove a lot of obstacles.

Create constant, consistent communication: After aligning the goals and strategies for innovation, create a consistent stream of communications from the executive leadership team to the business emphasizing the importance of innovation. This communication strategy needs to consider several audiences, including senior executives, individuals and teams responsible for innovation and the general employee population, and use a number of different channels and methods, including presentations, newsletters and other forms of communication to consistently reinforce the innovation message. These corporate communications exist to alert the entire company to new strategic directions and begin the task of changing the corporate culture. Your team may want to work with an internal communication resource and build a number of speaking points, FAQs, presentations, and other collateral to shape the discussions and the way the messages are delivered. Like voting in Chicago, the communication should happen early and often. Frequent, consistent communication sets a tone for the effort and alerts the entire organization that innovation is part of the strategic framework of the business and should receive specific focus from the teams.

The communication plan should plan for three phases. The first phase is targeted at the senior executives in the organization, to ensure they understand the purpose and strategy of the innovation initiative and team. It's important that they understand very early in the process how the team or innovation function will operate and how it will interface or impact any of the work their teams are currently doing. As an innovation leader, you'll want to manage these conversations face to face, with the innovation strategy and charter documents to frame the discussions. The second phase of communication targets the entire company, to introduce the concept of innovation and the purpose and rationale of an innovation capability or team. This communication should happen throughout the organization, initiated by a very senior officer, introducing the innovation team. The subsequent communications should then be conducted by the innovation team, to introduce the capabilities of the team and how anyone can get involved in innovation. These communications can use a range of channels, including email, web portals, discussion forums, posters, newsletters and other methods. Communication to groups or teams involved in a specific innovation program or task is the third phase of communication. In this regard, communication is targeted to a specific group for an idea campaign, brainstorm, or to address a specific opportunity or challenge. This communication must be carefully framed to enable the team to innovate effectively.

Timeframe:	Three to six months from the start of your innovation initiative
Deliverable:	A communication plan with key talking points distributed broadly throughout the organization, based on the agreed innovation charter
Responsible:	Innovation leader, innovation sponsor and internal communications team.

Change compensation schemes and encourage teams to work across organizational boundaries: Work with the leadership team and human resources to discuss how to change compensation to place more emphasis on innovation. Innovation is inherently risky and will be hard to manage and measure initially. Compensation plans provide subtle but very strong clues to employees as to the actions and accomplishments the management team believes are important and will reward. Employees will need to understand there are different "rules" for compensation and different definitions for success or failure associated with innovation. Your organization may need to make changes to compensation schemes to encourage teams to work across organizational boundaries and to encourage and reward more risk taking. This is not a simple task. It will require slow, gradual change as the innovation initiative unfolds, but it is an important change. If you cannot change the way people are rewarded and compensated, innovation will remain on the back burner as other, more important initiatives that are aligned with compensation arise.

Timeframe:	As soon as possible once the charter is complete
Deliverable:	Recommendations to encourage innovative behavior, rewards and compensation
Responsible:	Innovation leader and human resource executives

Some individuals will believe innovation "belongs" in their department or function. This will be especially true in a technology-focused company within product management or research and development. A lot of your success will depend on the definitions of innovation. If innovation is defined as exclusively product-centric and incremental, then you'll have a hard time reaching agreement that innovation is a broad-based effort that needs to exist outside of product management. The definitions that you've confirmed with the executive team and the scope of innovation will prepare you for these discussions. Probably the most important concept to convey is the structure, organization, and responsibility of the innovation team. In some instances, the innovation team will become a center of excellence for the entire organization. In other organizations, innovation may belong to one or more R&D groups or product groups. However innovation is structured, all business functions must understand how they benefit from the new structure or they will continue to work independently from the new innovation process. Think about the value your innovation program or initiative offers and how the executives and their teams benefit from your success.

Reach consensus and seek buy-in across the organization: Meet with the appropriate functional heads and line of business owners to understand their take on the ownership and importance of innovation in their function. Help them understand the position and purpose of the innovation team and seek opportunities to work together effectively. Where possible, offer to share tools, techniques and resources to improve innovation across the organization.

Timeframe:	As soon as possible once the charter is complete
Deliverable:	Meet with key executives whose functions or departments may be impacted by innovation to secure their buy-in
Responsible:	Innovation leader and senior executives

Finally, you'll need to define processes that cross organizational lines and create new working relationships. The actual design and implementation of those processes is defined later in this document, but you'll want to set the groundwork in this phase by demonstrating the importance of an integrated end-to-end process. You can do that by explaining the value of an innovation process and the role each function or line of business will play in that process. In many cases you may be able to call on respected internal resources like Six Sigma experts or organizational effectiveness consultants. Use existing process definitions as analogies for your innovation process. Every business has a number of clearly defined business processes that many people follow. Without an effective innovation process, sustainable, repeatable innovation is not possible. Just as everyone in your firm adheres to a specific purchasing process and does not create purchase orders outside of the defined process, innovation can become more profitable as it follows a consistent process.

More Reading/Resources

This topic, while especially important for innovation, is not unique to innovation initiatives. Any firm will suffer if its executive team is not cohesive and supportive of key initiatives. Probably one of the best books addressing these issues is *The Four Obsessions of an Extraordinary Executive* by Patrick Lencioni.

CREATING AN IDEA
MANAGEMENT PROCESS

Background

Every significant business function within your organization has a defined process or flow, whether that process is customer acquisition, purchase order creation, or product shipping. These processes define how work should be accomplished, the people necessary to complete the process, and their roles and responsibilities. For innovation to become consistent and sustainable in your organization, you must design and deploy a process and initiate a flow of ideas through the process that will produce new products and services. This "end-to-end" process should start from early ideation and trend spotting, and carry through to final product launch. Innovators need to understand how the process works and how ideas will travel through the process. Over the long term, the process itself becomes more important than an idea or the person who champions the idea.

In many firms today, innovation is not supported by a process, but is driven by individuals who identify interesting ideas for new products or services. These individuals adopt an idea and become "idea champions", pushing, pulling, and prodding the idea through an undefined series of decisions to attempt to create a new product or service. Some idea champions are well-suited for their roles due to their understanding of the organization, but few people have the breadth of knowledge and understanding of the formal and informal decision-making processes and cultural barriers to move an idea through the organization to become a new product. Using an "idea champion" approach to innovation is not scalable since so few people are able to create organizational buy-in and attract investment and resources to their ideas. Additionally, when just a few people "own" the generation and evaluation of ideas, you team will miss great ideas from others who don't have the moxie or stamina to become idea champions. There's simply no other important business function that has such a lack of definition as does innovation.

Now, many of you reading this are likely to say "We have a great process. We have a world-class capability to develop and launch new products". What we often find in many firms is a very poorly defined capability to generate, manage and evaluate ideas coupled with a powerful product development and launch capability, which is like pulling a freight train with a steam engine. Clearly in many firms there's a mismatch in capabilities in the "front end" of product and service development and the ability to develop and launch products. The entire process must work effectively for new products and services to be created consistently.

Case Study

Many of the firms we work with identify an innovation database as a key ingredient to success, but fail to recognize that the database itself doesn't add value. The value is in the process itself—the act of generating, capturing, and evaluating an idea. An end-to-end process includes inputs, actions, and outputs. Creating an idea database without defining the actions needed to generate and capture ideas on the front end, or defining how to evaluate and manage ideas on the back end, is doomed to failure. Idea databases that exist without defined processes will become information cul-de-sacs, and will be recognized as such by potential innovators. Few firms have a consistent, sustainable, effective process for managing ideas from early conception to final disposition as a new product or service, but all firms want to introduce new products and services consistently.

A large insurance firm evaluated a number of software alternatives and implemented an idea management software application to capture their ideas. However, the firm failed to build processes around the idea database to ensure ideas were constantly added to the database, and more importantly, that ideas were reviewed, discussed and evaluated and eventually moved on for further consideration by new product development teams. While the initial software deployment was considered a success, within a few months the number of ideas that entered the database dropped dramatically as people realized that the ideas were not being actively considered, and that few were moving on to new product development. The challenge for the company was not in capturing ideas but in defining a process to move those ideas to an evaluation stage and onward to new product or service development. Given the lack of a defined innovation process, there was no further action on the ideas after they were captured. The missing ingredient is a well-defined and well-understood process to do something with those ideas after they have been captured.

Importance of the process

Since most firms have well-defined business processes within all of their business functions, defining the innovation process would seem to be relatively easy. Ideas can be generated from a wide array of sources, and should move through a number of phases before reaching an approval step to become a new product or service. The ideas should be captured and exposed to more divergent thinking and review. Once the idea has been fully considered, it should be evaluated, and moved through prototyping, concept testing and possibly an early business-case stage before significant investment. Ideas should proceed through a series of decision points and move into new product development or new service development, then on to final evaluation and a market launch. These steps are simple to define on paper, but in reality are much more difficult to implement. Implementing a cross-functional business process with a wide array of stakeholders requires significant cultural change and the ability to obtain the "buy-in" of different teams with starkly different compensation schemes and agendas. Without a defined innovation process, ideas are managed by individual idea champions, who must create their own innovation process for each idea. While some firms have been successful in this approach, there are several significant challenges. First, requiring an idea champion to create his or her process for each idea wastes time and effort and increases the time from idea to new product launch. Defining a new process for every idea that's generated is an exceptionally inefficient way to identify and productize new ideas, considering that most organizations have optimized every other important process. No firm would seriously consider having each product team or functional area develop its own purchasing process or financial accounting approach. Second, idea champions are not scalable. At best, each person can sponsor only one or two significant ideas at a time, so anyone who takes on the role will carefully weigh the likely success of the project. There are few people who will have the skills, endurance, and desire to take on the challenge of championing an idea through a poorly defined or non-existent process. Without a defined process, your organization cannot scale its ability to generate and consider new ideas and most likely will discourage new innovators from promoting ideas. Third, idea champions cannot pass on their lessons learned and improve the process over time. There are no efficiency gains in this approach, so all ideas labor through an inefficient, redundant process, taking far too long to move towards becoming a new product or service. Defining a consistent idea management process for your company has other benefits as well. Innovation and new idea generation may happen in several distributed teams within your business. In fact, that's something your organization probably wants to encourage. The challenge that this distributed innovation creates is whether or not the teams use consistent processes and evaluation criteria to manage their ideas, or if they simply create "local" databases and idea processes. Your organization recognizes the value of consistent processes and systems for all other critical business functions. Why recreate the wheel for the one capability likely to drive organic growth?

As ideas mature through the process, your team will need to make decisions about these ideas based on some type of opportunity assessment and evaluation. These assessments indicate which ideas will be funded and moved forward as new products and services and which ones will be shelved or retained for further investigation.

Establishing a clear, consistent evaluation and assessment process will help the idea submitters understand how to organize their ideas and how the ideas will be judged. Opportunity assessment by a board or management team will require an examination of the breadth of ideas and opportunities, the resources at hand, the probability of success, and the impact of the success or failure of the idea. Part of the opportunity assessment may include a product or innovation portfolio, which documents the ideas and products that are currently under development. We'll examine the value of an innovation portfolio in a later chapter.

Challenges when the process is broken or missing

Without a defined process, it becomes unclear how to submit an idea and what will happen to an idea if it is submitted. Since people can't understand the process or "see it in action", they will be unwilling to submit ideas. Additionally, lack of a defined innovation process will create the following challenges:

- Each idea that is evaluated and worked on will require far more effort than if a defined process was in place

- Each person who works on innovative ideas will create their own innovation methodologies, rather than use a consistent process

- Each idea will be evaluated against a set of criteria generated specifically for that idea, but with no relevance to other ideas

- The approach will take longer than necessary, generate unnecessary information, and fail to answer all the relevant questions

- Innovation without a defined process is not scalable, not repeatable, and not sustainable

A final argument against informal idea management is that there is no method to capture the history, successes, and failures of the proposed innovations. In most firms these successes and failures become mythic stories that individuals tell each other and pass down from generation to generation, but often both the ideas and the failures are repeated. Without common processes, every new idea is an entirely new creation. Little history or best practice information is available to guide an idea champion to a successful conclusion. Additionally, many ideas are shelved not because they aren't great ideas, but because the timing is wrong. Any innovative firm will have scores of ideas that are strong, valid ideas waiting for the right market opportunity, technology introduction or other change in the market to bring the idea into action. An innovative firm will not only generate new ideas, but will constantly seek to invigorate old ideas.

Actions

Define an end-to-end process for innovation: Begin to define a process for any set of ideas—incremental product ideas or disruptive service ideas. Define how the ideas are generated, how and where they are captured, and who is responsible for moving the ideas to some evaluation stage. Determine how the ideas should be piloted or prototyped, and how they can be transitioned to a new product or new service development team. Create a "process map" for the end-to-end process, defining the tasks and actions that should be completed in each stage of the process. See an example process definition below. This example defines the information flow for one phase of the process—idea generation and early screening. It includes the flow of information, key decision points, documents and data created and the people involved in the process.

Next, exercise the process you've defined using one set of ideas. Identify and document the phases of the process that are difficult or uncertain, and revisit your process map to revise and correct the process. As your process matures, add more and different ideas to the process and roll out to different ideation groups.

Timeframe:	Three to four weeks
Deliverable:	A defined "end to end" process detailing the significant phases of the innovation process. Document the hand-offs, information generated, teams or individuals involved
Responsible:	Innovation team

Idea Process Flow Example

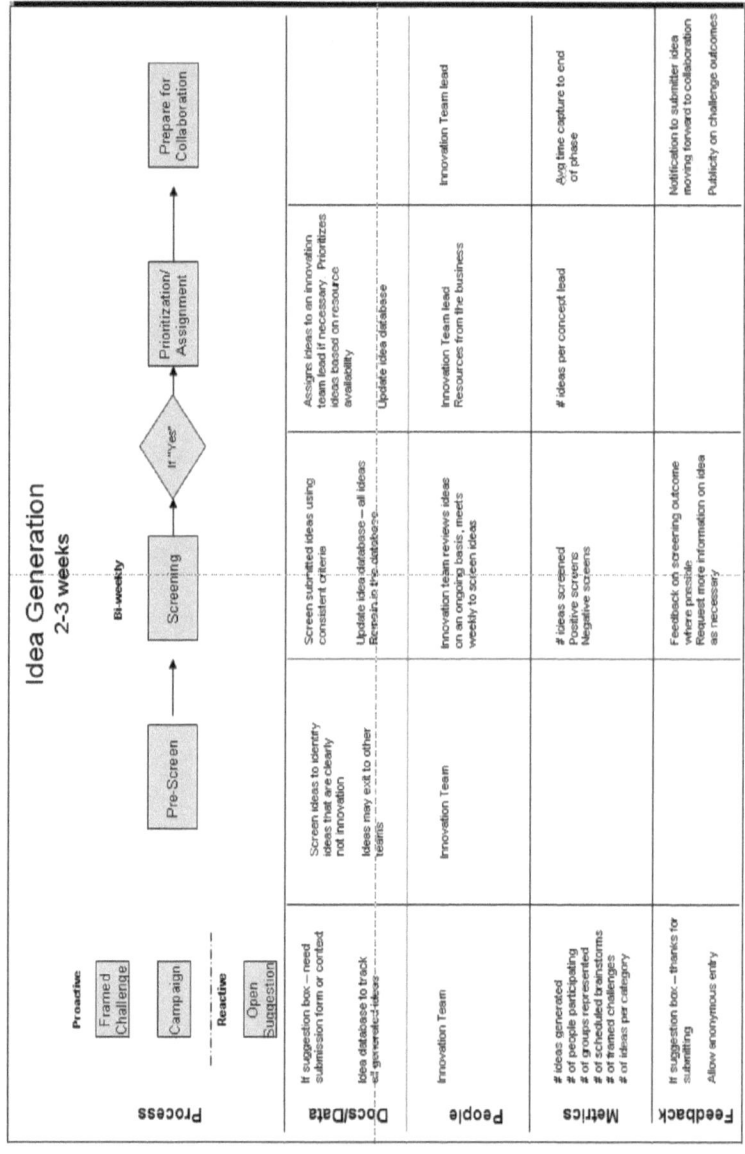

There are at least three significant challenges to defining and implementing an innovation process: First, there are few examples to follow. In many other business functions there are existing processes that can be leveraged or re-used. While your teams may currently be capturing and working ideas, most likely there are few scalable processes in their approaches. In many cases you'll need to define your innovation process from scratch. The good news is your firm is likely to have process management experts who can help you define and document the process. Second, capturing and managing ideas requires consistent communication and collaboration across business functions (sales, marketing, finance, etc.) that have different measurements and rationales for working on an idea. It will take time and focus to define the process and align the teams and the work to the process. Third, much of this work has to be accomplished initially by people who are available to assist with the innovation initiative in a part-time role, since they have other full-time responsibilities. Recognize that implementing an innovation initiative will take time and require a significant amount of collaboration, teamwork, and executive sponsorship. The process needs to be well-defined yet simple, since so few people will be fully engaged in the process.

Manage a small set of ideas and change the process as you learn: Define a single ideation process and communicate the value and importance of the process. Begin feeding ideas into the process, and ensuring those ideas are being evaluated and moved on for further consideration, or rejected for the "right" reasons. Meet with the heads of affected business functions to ensure they understand why their team members are being asked to consider and evaluate ideas. Focus on moving the initial ideas through the process on a timely basis with appropriate feedback to the idea submitters. Establish regular review cycles every two to three weeks to set the expectation that innovation will be managed as a sustained process. Document the steps of the process that are not clear or need further elaboration. Provide special oversight at the "handoffs" between two functions or responsibilities. Provide feedback on the outcome of the ideas to the individuals who submitted the ideas.

Consider the hand-offs of the ideas between the innovation team and the product or service development teams. In the "front end", ideation and idea generation can increase very quickly, and by defining good innovation processes, your firm can generate a significant number of new ideas very quickly. Unfortunately, if your organization does not align the ideas flowing to the development teams with the development organization's capabilities to accept and implement those ideas, a lot of good ideas will pile up, waiting to be evaluated and implemented by the development teams. When planning your innovation process, consider the importance of the handoff between the innovation team and the product or service development team. If the innovation team becomes more efficient and effective at creating and evaluating ideas, then the development teams must be ready to receive more ideas and convert more ideas to new products and services. Work to understand the bandwidth of the development processes and their ability to receive new product, service, and process ideas.

Timeframe:	During the innovation process definition
Deliverable:	Meetings and discussions with "downstream" processes such as new product development to understand and document the hand-offs from an "innovation team" to new product or service development.
Responsible:	Innovation team and product development

Focus on proactive innovation rather than reactive. In many cases an innovation team becomes a "catchall" for the ideas from across the company. While your team will want to encourage ideas and ideation, providing some focus on the important challenges or opportunities the business faces will help direct ideation into areas that are important and strategic. Your team can help itself and the organization by creating proactive ideation sessions that focus idea generation on opportunities, trends and threats that are relevant to the business. In this manner your team moves from a "reactive" posture to a proactive posture, gains ideas that are more in line with the expectations of the management team, and gathers ideas with greater impact. Additionally, proactive innovation has the additional benefit of generating ideas that align to the problem or opportunity you've identified. Open suggestion boxes or "reactive" innovation force the team to consider wildly different ideas, while proactive innovation defines a scope and context for the idea submitters. This simplifies evaluation and investigation of ideas as it limits to some extent the scope and breadth of the ideas submitted. Proactive innovation also ensures that the people in your organization are submitting ideas on topics or challenges that are of interest to your team and aligned to the strategic goals of the firm. Examples of proactive innovation include idea campaigns and "framed challenges" which seek ideas to respond to a specific opportunity, trend or threat.

Establish a consistent set of evaluation criteria. As ideas are generated and moved through an innovation process, it is important to consider how the ideas will be evaluated. Providing a consistent, transparent evaluation framework demonstrates that all ideas receive the same treatment and are managed in the same way. A clear, consistent evaluation framework communicates to individuals and teams who submit ideas how the ideas will be evaluated and what information is necessary in order for the ideas to be evaluated.

We've found the following evaluation criteria the most helpful in the firms we've worked with:

- How well does the idea **meet the needs of the customer or market**?

- How **important is the need** that is being met by the product or service?

- How **distinctive** is the idea in comparison to other offerings?

- How **valuable is the solution to the ultimate customer**?

- How **capable is the firm of creating the solution**, or finding a partner for the solution?

- How much will it cost and how much effort will it take to develop the idea?

- What is the potential return on investment of time and money in the idea?

Using the questions above as drivers, your team can create specific evaluation criteria for the ideas you generate. Each idea or idea category will require some questions or criteria that are unique to that idea or category. For instance, for some ideas, you may need to add evaluation criteria about any legal or regulatory issues involved. Developing these criteria as part of a consistent evaluation for the ideas that are generated ensures that all ideas are treated equally and can be compared once the evaluation is complete. Many firms will quickly convert these criteria to a set of quantitative results, based on metrics like ROI or hurdle rates. If ideas are treated like fixed assets too early in the process, most of them will be eliminated, since it takes time to investigate how the ideas can be deployed and what value they may provide. Don't discount the value of more qualitative data, such as management intuition or "gut" feelings. While we'd like innovation to be an exact science, there is a lot of value in the intuition of the management team as part of the evaluation. Don't base your decision-making on just a few numbers, without applying management intuition as well, at least early in the process. This process of opportunity assessment is probably one of the most important, but least understood concepts within firms that are struggling to become more innovative. Few successful innovations looked great initially and many seemed unlikely to ever return value. Where innovation is concerned, be sure to allow each idea enough runway to succeed or fail on its merits, and recognize that some ideas take longer to achieve recognition and acceptance than we'd prefer.

Timeframe:	Complete before ideas enter the innovation process
Deliverable:	A set of consistent evaluation criteria that can be applied to ideas that are presented to the team. Clearly there can be more than one set of criteria based on the types of ideas and their implementation.
Responsible:	Innovation team

More Reading/Resources

Many management consulting firms have developed innovation processes or methods and some firms have adopted these "canned" methodologies or developed internal methodologies or processes. Probably the best known new product development methodology is STAGE-GATE®. Some firms have adopted the STAGE-GATE® methodology for new product development and have extended its capabilities to provide an innovation process for the "front end". You can learn more about STAGE-GATE at www.stage-gate.com or find Robert Cooper's book, *Winning at New Products*.

OVO has developed its Concept to Cash™ methodology for innovation. You can read more about that innovation process here:

http://www.ovoinnovation.com/pdf/InnovateonPurpose2006.pdf.

Funding and Approval

Background

The challenge of innovation is not simply creating new ideas, but bringing them to market as new products and services as quickly and successfully as possible. One hurdle many teams face when developing new ideas is obtaining the funding to test or prototype an idea to determine its market viability. In most firms, new products are identified and then placed into a funding process that is incorporated into an annual operating plan. For a firm following a traditional calendar, this means that an initial budget is developed in June or July, with the final budget confirmed by November. Often the funds approved for the projects and products as part of the annual plan are not released until February or March the following year. Ideas that were generated and approved in the first quarter of one year may wait to receive funding to take to product development one year later. As innovators, we cannot expect the market and our competitors to wait for our new products and services to pass through a ponderous internal annual planning process. Clearly, some ideas which require major investments should pass through the annual plan. Ideally, however, the innovation team will have the funds necessary to move great ideas to market more quickly, using some of the same screens and considerations as the annual plan, but providing the funding for necessary research and development in a much more timely matter. After all, your customers and competitors don't care about your annual planning process, and many innovations have arrived on the market just after a competitor with a less onerous approval process introduces their version of the product or service. An annual planning process is a poor approach for evaluating and funding innovation initiatives. Annual planning and budgeting is focused on discrete products and services, with well defined return on investment. Most innovation projects or programs don't have the depth of detail or rigorous financial planning to survive the annual planning process, and many need to move more quickly than the plan will allow.

Some managers may question the need for further funding for ideas. Beyond the annual budgeting issue, there's another reason to consider the funding necessary to support innovation. While idea generation and evaluation is relatively inexpensive, activities relevant to maturing the idea require additional resources. Tasks such as concept development, market research, concept testing, building a prototype or pilot all require additional funds and require interaction with prospects and/or customers. These activities usually cannot be conducted by an internal team, and may require the involvement of consultants, business partners and your potential customers. Organizations with well-developed innovation capabilities provide "research and development" funds to ensure ideas do not stall in their development awaiting funding for these activities before the ideas are transferred to the appropriate teams for further development.

Case Study

A large consumer bank created an innovation team and implemented an idea management process which generated a number of new product and service ideas. However, since the innovation team lacked funds to prototype or test ideas, the team had to submit its ideas to an annual planning process for funding. The ideas suffered from two issues in the annual planning process. First, most ideas are not well-formed at this early stage, so determining measurements like return on investment for an idea was difficult with any degree of certainty. The annual planning process templates used financial measurements like ROI and hurdle rates to determine which ideas to fund. The planning team struggled to compare nascent ideas with little definition and projects that had detailed financial analysis. Innovative projects were frequently eliminated from consideration since it was so difficult to pinpoint a specific return. Second, even when the ideas were approved in the annual planning process, they did not receive funding for up to nine months after they were "approved", and in some cases over 14 months after the ideas were generated. This meant that the few ideas that were approved for funding were shelved until the funds were released or alternative funding mechanisms were identified. Without a consistent funding mechanism to provide resources to continue to develop and test the ideas that are generated, many valid ideas lay dormant until the funding cycle was completed or the team found other means to fund the most promising ideas. Meanwhile, more nimble competitors like Google, PayPal and banks were releasing new banking capabilities and innovations on a fast clip, able to speed new products to market through an innovation process more attuned to the demands of the market. The innovation team was unable in its original configuration to speed up the funding and approval of ideas, and recognizing the challenges, advocated innovation teams within the business units of the bank more closely associated with the product development cycles and funding cycles within each team.

Importance of Funding

Almost every idea your team generates will require some level of funding to flesh out the idea before it becomes a new product or service. That funding may be necessary to fuel more market research, help develop a business case for the idea, conduct preliminary trials, develop a prototype or fund other resources necessary to prepare the idea to become a new product or service. Innovation teams approach this challenge from several different perspectives:

- Some teams have an "Innovation Fund" that the innovation team uses to fund the activities necessary to continue to move an idea through the innovation process when the idea is not yet sponsored by any other entity. The innovation team does not need a lot of cash in order to accomplish its goals. Actions such as conducting market research or developing a simple prototype of an idea can move the idea through the innovation process a lot more rapidly with little investment. Many central innovation teams are successful funding additional research, concept development or testing on just a few hundred thousand dollars a year, speeding new products to market.

- Some teams seek sponsors for key ideas, or allow business units or business functions to submit or adopt ideas and provide funding for those ideas while the innovation team works the ideas and prepares them for future consideration. This shared responsibility provides the means for a central innovation team to move the idea through its paces more rapidly, while the sponsor organization provides funding for the team.

- Some firms, especially those in the high-tech market, use an approach similar to venture capital funding. Teams approach the venture board with concepts and ideas and pitch those ideas for funding just as they would to an external venture capitalist. This funding is provided as the idea matures and not in alignment with an annual planning process. Often the funds are distributed in tranches based on achievement to key milestones.

Regardless of your team's approach, funding the activities necessary to ripen and mature the ideas before implementation is important. Moving your ideas through the traditional budgetary or annual planning process commingles poorly defined and immature ideas with fully developed and defined projects, and makes the innovative ideas seem unworthy for further consideration.

Actions

As you begin your innovation initiative, there are two distinct needs for funding: funding for the team and resources necessary to start the innovation initiative, and funding for the ideas and the work necessary to evaluate, prototype, and prepare ideas for transition to products and services.

While a lot of your attention will be focused on the first funding concern— finding the money to form the initiative—you'll need to determine the best methods to fund ideas that are promising either as part of the annual planning process or through an innovation "R&D" fund.

Determine the costs necessary to organize and form the innovation initiative. In this effort, consider the roles, the people necessary, the processes, and the tools that must be in place for the effort to succeed and be sustainable. Simply identifying and attracting the people necessary to fill the roles to form the team and defining the processes can easily take 3 to 6 months. This work is primarily focused on setting up the initiative, and while some innovation work can be accomplished, the main goal during that timeframe is setting up the appropriate processes, team, and charter to define the innovation initiative and prepare for ideas to flow.

Determine how ideas will be funded as they move from concepts into potential products or services. As noted earlier, most firms establish a budget in the middle of the year for the following year. Few firms leave much flexibility to move funds around to promising new ideas that weren't in the annual plan. Additionally, the annual planning process can be a death trap for truly innovative ideas, because the measurements and metrics used to approve and fund ideas can be very stringent. Your team needs to reach an agreement with the management team on the proper approach for approving ideas as they move into a development or testing phase to determine if the annual planning process is the appropriate venue for ideas. Another method for funding ideas is to identify partners or other funding approaches from outside your organization. Some of these topics are covered in the chapter on Open Innovation later in the book.

Allocate funds for an innovation R&D budget. Your team will identify ideas that are very powerful and potentially rewarding, but won't be accepted by development teams and may not be ready to submit to a budgeting process. These ideas will wither and die without further research, testing or piloting, or further elaboration, which will require funding. An innovation team investment fund will enable your team to sponsor research, create a prototype and test it in the market, or conduct focus groups to confirm the design and validity of the idea.

Timeframe:	Within six months of the start of your initiative
Deliverable:	Confirmation on the method to allocate funds to ideas that are in work before an annual plan or instead of through the annual plan process.
Responsible:	Innovation leader and senior executives

DEFINING ROLES AND ALLOCATING PEOPLE

Background

People play an important role in innovation. The roles that people play within an innovation process are more important than in transactional processes such as purchasing or sales. There are several reasons why innovation demands more involvement and oversight than other processes. First, ideas are more fluid and intangible than purchase orders or financial closings. Early in the process ideas are very uncertain and only through evaluation and consideration do the ideas take definite shape. In most traditional business processes, people are called upon to manage exceptions, such as an order that is not approved or a delayed shipment. Where innovation is concerned, many of the ideas submitted will be eliminated from further consideration, so the "exceptions" are the ideas that remain. Each idea requires some involvement or oversight to move through the process. Second, innovation tends to involve many business capabilities and functions throughout the organization. At every stage in the process—idea generation, evaluation, testing, prototyping, and eventual development and launch, a wide range of people are involved in turning an idea into a new product, process, business model, or service. At some point, virtually every person in the company will have interaction with an innovation initiative, even if their role is only in idea generation. Third, innovation in many firms remains more of a craft than a defined process, so there is less process definition and system support for innovation, requiring more personal attention to the subject. Ideas usually aren't well defined early in the process, so they can't be evaluated and managed by systems or technologies. People have to be involved given the uncertainties and gray areas related to innovation.

While people are very important for innovation to succeed in your firm, selecting the "right" people can make all the difference. Some people will naturally gravitate to innovation, since it has the aura of creativity and newness, and is unlike their regular, more mundane jobs. However, to be effective, innovation must exist within a set of processes and guidelines, and people must play important roles aligned to the innovation process. Otherwise the system becomes a cul-de-sac where ideas are captured, but never evaluated or implemented.

The impact of HR

Culture is more important than creative, innovative individuals when it comes to innovation. Evidence demonstrates that a culture that sponsors innovation is much more likely to create successful new products and services than a firm with innovative individuals but limited cultural acceptance of innovation. The impact of people and culture on the ability of the firm to innovate can't be overstated. Since culture is so important, an underappreciated team within your organization—human resources—may hold a key to helping your team become more innovative. Human resources teams control the three "R's" necessary to grow an innovative culture—recruitment, retraining, recognition.

To create an innovative culture and align people to the correct roles to support innovation, the "right" people need to be recruited to your team. In the last decade, recruiting has focused on individuals with excellent operational skills, those who can improve efficiency or cut costs. Many of these people may be able to innovate, but they were not hired for those particular skills. Traditional recruiting methods and job descriptions have eliminated people who are more creative or innovative, as their skill sets don't have a lot of overlap with those who are more focused on operational excellence. The Human Resources team needs the direction from your senior management team to start recruiting people who bring more innovative skills to the team. This new focus may also include recruiting people who have skills or perspectives that are new or different from the existing team, to encourage new thinking. Beyond recruiting, the HR team can impact the culture and help define roles for innovation by retraining the existing workforce. In most firms, you can't simply recruit a brand new team, but will work with the people you have. Training on creative thinking, innovation, and new approaches to problem solving can impact the way people think, and will indicate to the existing team that innovation is important. Finally, HR can help shape the way people are recognized and rewarded for their efforts. If we place a significant emphasis on innovation, but don't change the way people are recognized for their efforts or compensated, they'll continue to do what they've always done. As we define new roles, the individuals filling those roles need new training and a different compensation structure, or they'll return to working in the way they've always worked. You need to enlist the services of your HR team to help you as your innovation initiative unfolds.

Roles

The roles necessary for innovation to succeed are dependent on the definition of your innovation process, and the breadth and depth of your innovation needs. The "end-to-end" idea management process will define a number of roles—from idea generation and facilitation to idea evaluation and business case development. Some of these roles may be full-time roles, but there are also a number of occasional, part-time roles for individuals involved in idea generation and brainstorming, and roles tied to managing the ideas through a process and evaluating and maintaining a portfolio of ideas as an ongoing concern. The roles as we've defined them assume a centrally managed innovation initiative that sponsors innovation in various lines of business and business functions in the business, where ideas are generated and evaluated. Another reason to consider Human Resources as a valuable aid during the development of your innovation initiative is that many of the roles for innovation don't currently exist in your business, and will need to be defined before they can be filled.

Case Study

In our consulting efforts, the most common question we receive as we define the work necessary to manage ideas more effectively is: Who is going to do this work? Without careful consideration of the roles and responsibilities, innovation will fail quickly. As we identified above, your organization can rely on one innovation champion to force the idea through the organization, or set up a process where different people participate in the idea along the process in certain well-defined roles. In a number of clients we've established a "corporate" or central innovation team, whose role is to define and to sponsor processes, tools, and techniques to promote innovation throughout the organization. This small team works collaboratively with individuals and teams from business units, product teams, and business functions to create new ideas and evaluate the ideas. Within the central team we usually define three key roles:

- Trend gathering and analysis: While trends, competitive data and market research are often generated throughout the organization, there are few people who have a responsibility to organize that information and synthesize it. The corporate innovation team can provide that capability as an input to new ideation.

- Process manager: Providing a common innovation platform—tools and processes—is one of the key goals. Within the corporate innovation team, a person should be responsible for defining and managing the innovation processes, and training other teams to use the process effectively.

- Idea Coach or Facilitator: In some instances the corporate innovation team may need to provide assistance during an innovation project, or train a team in innovation tools or techniques. Additionally, some ideas may need more oversight or nurturing from the corporate innovation team. In this regard, the idea coach or facilitator can play an important role.

- Other important roles include managing communications to the organization about the role and purpose of the innovation initiative, and developing training programs to help seed innovation agents throughout the organization.

These roles support the idea through a process and ensure a number of people participate to capture and manage the idea effectively. Outside of the central team, innovators may also hold positions or roles in business units or business functions. These innovators may recognize a new opportunity or generate a new, valuable idea and form an initiative or team to help mature the idea into a new product or service. While the corporate or central innovation team represents a permanent position, these "local" innovation roles are created for the life of the innovation initiative and then the individuals return to their "regular" jobs or follow the new products or services.

Importance of People in the innovation process

As with any process or workflow, people take on different roles and responsibilities in different phases of innovation. Early in the process, people will be called on to generate ideas through brainstorming, trend evaluation, or from inferring customer wants and needs. Some people will prioritize these ideas and capture them for further consideration. Other people may contribute additional details or information about an idea, and a group or team will evaluate ideas based on documented criteria. Generally speaking, the roles we've defined so far should be held by different people, probably in different business functions or departments. If only one small team generates, manages, and evaluates all ideas, their ideas are likely to become too narrow and miss a number of opportunities. Additionally, in a small team there's a significant opportunity for groupthink. The roles within the process should be held by people with an interest in the idea, but also by people who can review and evaluate an idea objectively, and by individuals with responsibility for funding the idea or launching the new idea. Clearly a successful innovation initiative will impact a broad number of people who will play a wide range of roles throughout the process.

As noted, there are a number of roles in an innovation process. These include idea generators, trend watchers, people who gather and analyze customer needs, people or teams who evaluate ideas, people who develop the product or service, people involved in the financial evaluations and considerations of the product, and people responsible for the launch. Each of these individuals plays an important part of the innovation process, and must understand their role and its relationship to the innovation process.

If the process is driven by people, then we ought to consider what motivates them. In most firms, people are driven by their compensation, recognition, feedback, opportunities for advancement, and the direction set by their management team. To encourage people to work on a sustainable innovation program, you'll want to identify the benefits they'll receive by taking the time to work on the ideas and the innovation process, provide feedback on the successes and failure of the process and what's been learned, and ensure the management team is providing a lot of consistent public support for your innovation initiative. Individuals who participate in innovation initiatives must understand that their involvement in innovation is viewed positively by the company and that the innovation efforts are important. Consistent communication, management involvement, and changes in compensation and recognition must be applied as the innovation initiative is rolled out to the team—otherwise the initiative will lack credibility and people will not participate. You'll need to demonstrate that people can succeed and advance working in an arena that is very public and has a higher than normal occurrence of failure, as any innovation initiative should.

Identifying Challenges with People in Innovation

There are several signs that your innovation initiative is struggling based on the people assigned to the task or their roles. These include: poor communication, mismatched compensation and objectives, lack of commitment to the innovation process, and uneven application of the innovation process.

If the process lacks a defined set of roles that map to the process, then the ideas will not "flow" through a process but will become "stuck" in specific phases of the process. The individuals who are responsible for these steps in the process may not understand their roles due to poor training, or may not be committed to the innovation process because their loyalties (and compensation) lie with other jobs or other business functions. Another problem that can arise springs from bias about the ideas and where they were generated, causing uneven consideration of the ideas. The innovation team needs to consider all ideas equally until the first evaluations are completed. Frequently teams will reject an idea out of hand because of its source or a rash prediction of its likely outcome. This leads to a lack of confidence in the people and the process.

The final problem that can arise is the concept of the idea "champion"—a person who ignores the stated processes and methods and attempts to commercialize an idea with no involvement from the innovation team. While this approach may on occasion be successful, it is not an optimal approach as it does not provide for a measurable, defined process and it detracts from the work the innovation team attempts to do by creating a consistent process.

Actions

Recruit your human resources team: Innovation, more than any other process, is driven by creative, engaged people. People are especially important early in the development of your innovation initiative, since there will be few processes or systems to rely on. People are important in the generation of ideas, the evaluation of ideas and the eventual launch of the ideas, and people play an important part of the innovation life cycle. Bringing the Human Resources team into the picture as early as possible, defining the requirements for people and the impacts on the culture of the organization, will help smooth the way for your initiative.

Timeframe:	As soon as the charter is finalized
Deliverable:	Meet with the HR team to identify key needs and to help shape the culture and compensation and reward systems
Responsible:	Innovation leader and HR senior executives

Select the "right" people. Innovation requires a different set of skills than working in a traditional business process. Your team needs people who can bring a unique set of skills that may not be as appreciated in other parts of the business. Emphasize synthesis over analysis and the ability to live within a very ambiguous space. Identify creative people with disparate backgrounds and disciplines, and focus especially on those individuals who are great communicators. Your team will work well when it is willing to consider a wide range of ideas and to stretch each idea to its limit. Doing so will require great communication skills within the team and with the rest of the organization. However, your innovation team must understand its importance and place in the organization. While these skill sets are important for innovation success, the team must demonstrate an ability to work within specific guidelines and align to the strategic plans of the business. Just as Myers-Briggs helps people understand how they interact with others, there is a simple assessment to evaluate an individual's perspective and proclivity for innovation. The Kirton Adaption Innovation (KAI) assessment evaluates whether one has a preference as an adaptor or innovator. Kirton's definition of an innovator is a person who is "less tolerant of structure (guidelines, rules) and less respectful of consensus. An adaptor has more respect for rules and structure. He prefers to solve problems in a defined environment, working to do things "better" as opposed to breaking the paradigms.

As part of your evaluation and selection of people to play important roles in your innovation initiative, you may want to test people for their perspectives about innovation using the KAI assessment.

Another tool or assessment to use to encourage diversity and breadth on your innovation team is the FourSight Thinking Assessment. This assessment indicates the preferences of the individuals on the team and breaks them into four categories—clarifiers, ideators, developers and implementors. It's important for a well balanced innovation team to have people who have strengths in all four of these areas. A number of consulting firms offer the FourSight Assessment of your team in person or even online.

Timeframe:	As soon as possible after the charter is finalized
Deliverable:	Identify the skills and capabilities necessary to support innovation and begin to identify the appropriate people within your organization
Responsible:	Innovation leader and senior executive

Build and educate your innovation team: Identify the people you'll need to make the innovation process work effectively. Initially it may be more important to identify people who are interested in innovation and idea management, rather than the "right people" within each function. At first it's more important to demonstrate results. Identify the roles you expect people to play within the innovation process and help them understand the importance of the role. Build innovation training programs or identify third party training programs to introduce more creative thinking and innovation techniques to your team. A suggested curriculum will include training for individuals on individual competencies like creative thinking and group facilitation, and for group skills on teamwork, process definition, conflict resolution, working in ambiguity and other competencies. Work with the management team and human resources department to change the compensation scheme to encourage participation in the innovation process. Finally, provide feedback. Let the team know what's working and what's not working and the results of their efforts.

Timeframe:	As you build your team
Deliverable:	Define the roles within the innovation team and the training necessary to help each team member become accustomed to their new roles
Responsible:	Innovation leader and HR team

Evolve the job responsibilities as your team grows and gains experience: As the team matures and the process becomes more defined, document the important roles and responsibilities that support and enable innovation to create established roles for innovation. Document the early successes and failures to provide learning for teams that follow yours.

Team structure: Innovation initiatives take time to unfold and require a significant amount of work, at the corporate level as well as within a business unit or business function. People who are interested in working on innovation initiatives need to understand their roles and understand the management commitment and timeframes they have to work within to achieve a successful outcome. From the outset, a corporate innovation team that defines tools, techniques, and processes should contain several full-time roles, while innovation teams within a product group or business unit may form and disband as the ideas are generated and evaluated.

More Reading/Resources

Probably the best known resource on people, roles and innovation is Tom Kelley's book *The 10 Faces of Innovation*. In this book Kelley examines the types of people who are necessary for innovation to succeed, including learning personas, organizing personas and building personas. His book provides a great overview into the types of people you need to succeed in an innovation initiative.

Adaption-Innovation by Michael Kirton explains some of the theory behind the differences in the way people perceive innovation and how they participate in an innovation task.

Ruth Ann Hattori and Joyce Wycoff, the founders of the Innovation Network, wrote a training guide for innovation called *Innovation Training* that covers skill sets for individuals as well as team and includes a number of exercises.

Developing a culture
of innovation

Background

In many firms, innovation is viewed as creating new products or introducing successful upgrades of existing products. Therefore, innovation is often thought of as the responsibility of product development and/or research and development. In these cases, innovation is housed in R&D or product management, and few ideas are captured and evaluated outside of these teams on a regular basis. While this is a perfectly valid definition of one kind of innovation, it is a very narrow view of innovation. Everyone within your firm is capable of generating valuable ideas, and those ideas can reflect much more than new or upgraded physical products. In fact, if your organization is not actively generating and implementing new ideas in areas such as new services, new business models or new channels, then you are missing a significant number of opportunities. The US economy is predominantly based on services rather than manufacturing—over 80% of our GDP is generated in services. If the focus of your innovation initiative is solely or predominantly product innovation, your firm is missing a significant number of opportunities. Additionally, ideas can come from individuals or groups outside your organization—your customers, your partners, and your vendors. Taking a larger view, it's easy to see that innovation should involve the entire organization. This view, however, will require a shift in the way your organization thinks about innovation and who is responsible for innovation. You'll need to change your culture to broaden the responsibility for innovation and ensure everyone participates and understands the importance and value of innovation.

The cultural shift begins by changing the concept that innovation "belongs" to one team, and encouraging everyone to participate. The shift involves moving from a "not my job" mentality, or worse, a "not invented here" mentality, to a state where ideas are generated frequently, discussed openly, shared and improved through collaboration, and quickly moved to become new products or services.

A cultural shift is also necessary in many firms due to the recent emphasis on process excellence and cost cutting. In the decade of the 90s and beyond, many firms have implemented programs intended to reduce costs and risks. The corporate cultures that formed around these principles value consistency and repeatability over risk taking. This management paradigm must change if the organization is to adopt and embrace an innovation culture. Innovation requires a willingness to experiment with new methods and approaches. A prevailing culture that is focused on process excellence and repeatability will quickly stamp out innovation efforts unless the culture is changed through management direction and involvement, consistent communication and new compensation models.

Cultural acceptance of an innovation imperative is probably the most important factor for long-term innovation success.

Case Study

In a large insurance firm we've worked with, new ideas were generated by a small team of people who identified the ideas, evaluated the ideas, and then worked to shape the ideas into new products or services. When the demand for new ideas was relatively small, this approach worked well, except for a lack of consistent communication and shared processes. However, when the demand for innovation increased, the approach proved to be difficult to scale. The existing culture of the group played an important role in those difficulties. In the existing model, each person became the champion of one idea and did not communicate its strengths or weaknesses to other team members. There was little incentive to share information or to use common processes. Team members selected the ideas they preferred to work on and rarely interacted with other team members. After some initial success, the number of ideas increased and management became interested in which ideas were receiving attention and in the efficiency and effectiveness of the team. At that point the existing cultural attitudes toward teamwork, collaboration, and communication slowed the acceptance of innovation more broadly.

The team reconvened under new operating principles that encouraged collaboration on ideas, group evaluation and input, and broader decision-making on which ideas should receive time and attention. Under these new principles the team was able to manage and evaluate many more ideas and speed the conversion of ideas into new products and services.

Importance of Culture

If your product management teams or R&D teams have grown to think of themselves as the "innovation" engine, they may well be threatened by the creation of an innovation initiative that's not controlled within their team. They may believe the creation of an innovation team threatens their autonomy or control of innovation, or reflects the feeling that their work has been inadequate. However, since ideas are sourced from many different individuals and locations, product management or R&D cannot hope to capture, manage, and evaluate ideas from so many different sources. Additionally, R&D does not have the experience or expertise to evaluate and make decisions on ideas that reflect business model changes or new services. As the innovation manager, you'll need to provide an excellent rationale for the individuals who "own" product innovation, and help them to understand their role is still vital to the success of the organization.

Cultural norms drive what people do and what they are expected to do. If your culture expects and embraces innovation, accepts risk-taking, and understands failure is part of the innovation process, then the people within the culture will participate in innovation initiatives. The cultural attitudes must filter down from the top—innovation teams can quickly identify whether or not senior management is supportive of innovation by the messages they send through communication channels or the way they allocate resources. Placing an emphasis on innovation and changing the culture to embrace innovation needs to start at the top.

Finally, it's interesting to note we often speak of managing innovation, but rarely of managing *for* innovation. The first concept has to do with managing ideas and processes, but the second concept has to do with how we enable people and teams to explore ideas and expand their horizons. Many managers are very comfortable with the first concept, but there's much less commitment for the second concept. Only as executives and managers demonstrate they are willing to change their organizational cultures and management styles to manage for innovation will the capability take root.

Challenges of Culture

We hear quite frequently "we just aren't very innovative here" or "we have a strong 'not invented here' (NIH) mentality". These are symptoms of a culture that will resist innovation. Culture is probably the most powerful force of all of the ones we've identified, and takes the longest to change. No matter how strong your innovation processes are, if the culture of the organization is not prepared for or simply does not believe in innovation, your innovation initiatives will fail. Signals that the culture is not ready to embrace innovation include:

- Fear of submitting ideas

- Fear of failure and consistent risk avoidance

- Lack of participation in innovation events and processes

- Lack of commitment from senior leaders

- Lack of cooperation from other business units or business functions

- Focus on the urgent, quarterly results at the expense of innovation

A great idea can work its way through any organization—regardless of its culture or support for innovation—if the idea is compelling enough and has vocal, energetic champions. The importance of a supportive culture can't be overstated, however. Culture is consistently indicated as the biggest stumbling block to generating more ideas and implementing them successfully. If your firm seeks to innovate consistently, you must focus on the changes necessary to make your corporate culture more welcoming to innovation.

Actions

Establish the breadth of the innovation initiative. There are really two actions here that are intertwined. First, you need to establish how broadly an innovation focus should be deployed in your business. Should service improvement ideas be considered? Where should those ideas be sourced? Should all product teams and lines of business generate and submit ideas? Determine which teams can source ideas and who should manage and evaluate ideas. The broader the scope of the ideas, the more people involved and the greater the impact on the culture. Second, you'll need to communicate these changes to the existing "innovators" in a way that includes them, but helps them understand the changes underway. Early, consistent communication from the innovation team and from the executive team is important.

Next, you'll want to create a common language, framework, and process for the entire company to use. This will help create a common approach for innovation regardless of the source of the idea or who evaluates the idea. This will also create a community of innovators who can interact and add more credibility to the innovation culture. As people adopt the same approach to and language for innovation, they'll reinforce the same thinking and culture.

Create a common approach through communication and training: Create a training program that defines your organization's definitions of innovation and a common innovation language, and also provides a program to introduce innovators to the common innovation process. Identify innovators who are willing to work across functional and team barriers, and train them using the curriculum and training program you've defined. In this way you will create a community of innovators who can then reinforce the best practices and processes your firm creates. Train them in these innovation process building blocks and tools, and become a resource for these innovators. This approach will help establish a much more consistent innovation approach throughout the organization.

Timeframe:	As your innovation initiative unfolds
Deliverable:	Create a common innovation process and develop training to support that process so others within the organization can understand. Define consistent methods, approaches and terms to create a consistent "language" for innovation.
Responsible:	Innovation team and HR team

Ensure your management team walks the talk: Merely setting up an innovation team and establishing an innovation process is not enough. If the management team does not fully support innovation initiatives through their communications, their priorities and their actions, no amount of cultural change will result in a successful innovation initiative. Where possible, demonstrate what the management team needs to do, in terms of communication, priorities, staffing, funding, and participation in order to demonstrate their commitment. One of the best ways to ensure the management team "walks the talk" is to have them model the behavior you want from the rest of the organization. Get the management team involved in early idea generation and evaluation so that the rest of the organization can see their involvement and understand that the management team supports the work.

Your goal through these actions is to change the corporate culture to create an expectation that everyone should have some involvement in innovation. This involvement may require a range of involvement—from encouraging individuals to submit ideas during a brainstorm or idea generation campaign to assigning a team to evaluate an idea. By creating a common approach and training innovation leaders, you can disseminate the knowledge of innovation approaches and establish a common innovation framework across your organization. Be realistic about this cultural change—it will require several years to fully embed a "culture of innovation" in any organization. When you embark on this effort, ensure the management team understands the timeframes and has reasonable expectations. Innovation can provide some "quick hits", but a sustained innovation process requires a culture that embraces innovation, which will take time to implement.

Examine corporate compensation and recognition: Most people are motivated by the recognition and compensation they receive, as well as by the intrinsic value of the work they do. To change the culture to promote innovation, people within the firm need to understand that they will be recognized and rewarded for their efforts, and not punished for the failures which will occur with innovation. Your team will need to work with Human Resources on new compensation options, rewards, and corporate recognition, and the celebration of innovation successes and failures. Asking people to commit their time and effort on innovation initiatives without changing their compensation or evaluation metrics is doomed for failure. The compensation and evaluation programs that exist for them will drive their participation and involvement.

Timeframe:	As you build your innovation team
Deliverable:	Review and change the compensation structure to encourage more risk taking.
Responsible:	Innovation team and HR team

Recognize and reward success *and* failure: It's expected that your management team will reward success. Recognizing and rewarding failure, or at least not punishing those who have attempted to innovate within the approved processes and methods, will demonstrate that the management team expects people to innovate. The reaction to the success and/or failure of a project will create more cultural change that just about any other action your organization can take.

Timeframe:	Anytime, any opportunity
Deliverable:	Recognize the actions and efforts of the innovation team. Celebrate success and recognize the effort if the innovation fails
Responsible:	Innovation lead, sponsor and HR

More Reading/Resources

Scott Berkun has an excellent book called the *Myths of Innovation* in which he examines some of the key challenges to innovation in business. Chapters 4 (People love new ideas), 6 (Good ideas are hard to find) and 8 (The best ideas win) point out areas where the culture impacts the ability of the firm to generate and manage ideas and the cultural bias that exists against innovation.

Robert Tucker's *Driving Growth through Innovation* has a chapter on culture that outlines some other ideas and actions you can take to change the corporate culture.

Changing the
Organization Chart

Background

Over the last 10 years the focus in many firms has been on slimming down, right-sizing and outsourcing work that can be done more effectively by other companies to find the firm's "core" strengths. This strategy produced lean firms and improved results, but it also produced firms that don't necessarily have the organizational structure or capacity to grow organically. Most firms are organized into vertical stovepipes consisting of product groups or lines of business, and cross-hatched by strategic processes. While innovation is identified as an important component for growth and differentiation, it does not clearly fit within this operating structure. Innovation can occur in any product group, business function, geography or vertical, and requires an end-to-end process to mature an idea into a new product or service. Other than within R&D or product management, there have been few organizational models for new product or service consideration. Traditional organizational models aren't helpful in this regard either. The traditional organizational structure—marketing, sales, finance, and product lines or business units—was formed to improve throughput and management of existing products, eliminate costs, and increase efficiency. These organizational structures are in many ways antagonistic to the needs of innovation. There are few organizational structures in most firms to support a consistent innovation initiative, so a firm seeking to become more innovative will need to consider its organizational structure to ensure there are no significant barriers to an innovation initiative, and determine if changes are necessary to improve how innovation works within the firm.

Case Study

In many organizations we work with, the question isn't whether the organization should be innovative, but where innovation should take place. In most large organizations, innovation is taking place within a number of innovation "locations" throughout the business:

- Within a product group, within R&D

- Across several product groups or lines of business

- In the "white space"

- With a business partner or customer

- As an individual, using time approved by the company for free exploration (e.g. Google, 3M and others set aside 10% of their employees time to investigate new ideas)

All of these locations are important and valid. The question becomes, how should your company organize itself for effective innovation in these different locations? Clearly innovation should happen in each of these locations, and for the greatest benefit should be sponsored and managed through standard techniques, tools, and processes. Many firms are turning to a central innovation team, which helps provide common tools and frameworks for ideas managed within product groups, and can take on the creation and management of ideas in the "white space". This organizational concept addresses several issues. First, the structure allows innovation to occur in small, local teams rather than in the central team. The central team's primary responsibilities are to provide sponsorship, resources, and common platforms to the teams that are innovating. Second, the central team can take on ideas that are too risky or too immature for a product group or line of business to consider. Third, the central innovation team provides increased visibility for ideas in process, and reduces rework and redundancy. A corporate innovation team provides a lens to view innovation across the business, and a team to house ideas that are exceptionally risky or have long maturity cycles that might not be workable within a traditional product team or business function. The corporate innovation team defines and sponsors innovation tools, processes, and techniques and helps product groups and business units become more proficient, and more consistent, at their innovation tasks. Fourth, a central team can encourage and foster collaboration across innovation teams and projects in different business units or profit centers. This collaboration will increase the capabilities of both organizations, reduce redundancy and rework and provide new perspectives on ideas or avenues to partner to create entirely new products or services. Fifth, the central innovation team can gather information on active innovation projects and publish an innovation pipeline or portfolio, which will indicate the types of innovation projects and identify any gaps in the innovation strategy.

Importance of Organization

From an organizational perspective, there are at least three significant factors to consider when your firm seeks to become more innovative:

1. The types of ideas to be generated and how they align to strategic goals

2. Who should "own" and evaluate those ideas

3. Where those ideas should be worked and where the skill sets reside

Let's look at each of these factors in more detail. The type of ideas that must be generated dictate the span and scope of innovation and ties back to an earlier discussion on defining an innovation charter. If the innovation strategy is to focus on incremental product ideas, then much of the "innovation" in your business will happen in product management departments, leaving a lot of the great ideas out of the mix. However, if your firm's innovation strategy includes disruptive ideas, service or business model ideas, the people involved in generating and implementing those ideas don't belong just to R&D or to product management. How your organization defines innovation will drive the type of ideas that are encouraged and who will work on those ideas, and who "owns" the idea. The definition of innovation will dictate the scope and breadth of the team that needs to be involved for innovation to succeed.

Regardless of the origin of the ideas, they will need to be considered and evaluated by individuals from a wide range of functional groups. A new product idea conceived by the product management team still requires evaluation from Sales, Marketing, Legal, Finance, and a range of other individuals and functions. You must consider who needs to interact with an idea and when and how that interaction should take place over the course of the idea's development. Additionally, you must consider how the idea moves from team to team, and whether or not the structure or process exists to sponsor the idea across functional or geographic barriers. These evaluations are recorded and available to other innovators and other teams, to ensure a consistent evaluation and to keep the evaluators honest in their assessments of the idea and its feasibility.

Also, given that innovation is a new focus in many businesses, you'll want to consider whether or not the skills exist across the organization to innovate consistently. Some product groups or lines of business may have the resident skills to improve products and services, while others, for example, have a cost-cutting focus and may struggle with innovation. Ideas should be evaluated and managed by the organization that will be responsible for creating and launching the new product or service, but some teams may need help improving their innovation techniques.

Given these three challenges, we often recommend a corporate-level innovation team or resource group which will be the repository of innovation techniques, tools, and processes. We recognize that this group's title and location on the org chart are important, and that adding a new team or new function within your organization may be problematic. What is important is to create a small team of people who can provide enterprise-wide innovation capability and plant the seeds to improve innovation in any team, product group, or business function. This group provides the training, tools, and processes to product groups, lines of business or business functions, and coaches the innovation teams within those groups.

Working in this manner serves several purposes:

1. Housing the team at the corporate level—that is, outside of a specific product group or line of business—ensures visibility into all innovation teams and promotes collaboration and consistency in language, tools, and approach across the entire organization. The level of reporting also indicates the importance the executive team places on the innovation effort, and the expected breadth and scope of innovation within the firm. If the innovation team reports to R&D or Product Management, the unspoken meaning is that innovation should primarily focus on product developments and enhancements.

2. A small core of innovation advocates, consultants or coaches can provide skills and techniques to the organization without each function or business

unit needing to add these skill sets that may not be used day-to-day in the business.

3. The corporate innovation team can sponsor ideas and work with team members, but the ideas belong to and are housed in the business unit or function where they will be realized, so ownership does not become an issue.

4. The corporate innovation team can nurture ideas that don't have a clear sponsor. "White space" ideas that don't clearly belong to one product group or line or business, or are too controversial or disruptive for objective evaluation within a product group or line of business, can be housed initially within the corporate innovation team. Many product lines and business units simply don't have the manpower or patience to evaluate ideas that may take several quarters or more to mature. Additionally, the corporate innovation team can provide assistance managing ideas that require the involvement of two or more competing product teams or business functions.

Clearly, a company focused on innovation must consider how it organizes itself to sponsor ideas and move them through a process. Current organizational structures don't promote innovation, and require more overhead than is necessary. A few small changes to your organizational chart may make a large difference in how quickly you become more innovative.

Other structures

In many traditional R&D organizations, a venture team may be a credible alternative. Firms like Intel and Medtronics use venture teams to evaluate a small set of ideas and determine their validity. The venture team consists of a scientist, a junior general manager, and several other individuals. The venture team is responsible for sifting through a small set of product ideas, generating more of their own, and determining if any of the ideas can be implemented as a new product or service. The venture team has only a few people, but does have a budget to pay for the resources it needs in order to research and develop ideas. If the team determines an idea has merit, the team will develop a business case and present it to a venture board to request further funding. If the board approves the funding, the general manager takes on the responsibility to grow the product line and the scientist returns to foster more creativity. This approach assumes that the ideas are well-developed and can be quickly converted into new physical products that are adjacent to existing applications or completely new applications. This approach also assumes that there are existing processes and methods in place, and that the initial funding to complete any necessary research is available.

In the book *Payback: Reaping The Rewards of Innovation*, authored by James P. Andrew, Harold L. Sirkin, and John Butman discuss a third approach. At Citigroup, a new position was created called the Innovation Catalyst. One Innovation Catalyst had responsibility for an innovation process in a country or region. Thus, the structure of the organization included a new, senior executive who championed innovation locally and had access to funding and other resources to identify and promote great ideas. The Innovation Catalyst helped to shape ideas, promote them internally and find the resources necessary to bring them to market.

In your organization, you may have examples of all three of these types of organizational structures or methods—a central team to sponsor and manage innovation, and different organizational models in the product groups and business units. Regardless of the organizational structure that is best for your business, supporting the innovation activities and processes with an intentional organization focused on improving innovation performance will strengthen the firm's ability to innovate and reinforce an innovation culture.

Challenges with Organization

There are several challenges to consider when considering the right organizational structure for innovation. First, innovation can and should happen in a number of locations throughout your business. New product development, research and development, business units and functional areas may all consider new ideas. This is normal and should be encouraged. The question becomes how to best organize these disparate teams. Second, innovation may be considered as a distributed responsibility or a centrally managed responsibility. In either case, we advocate a central team to help establish consistent methods, processes and approaches. A central team may present a cultural challenge to the organization and should be introduced carefully, its expectations and scope clearly defined. Without a clear organizational strategy, however, each team or "location" will determine its appropriate staffing, roles and responsibilities for an innovation team. This will lead to duplication of effort, poor alignment of skills and capabilities and understaffed and undermanned teams creating duplicative systems and processes. Defining the appropriate organizational structure for innovation and sponsoring innovation from the top down can speed innovation and simplify the organizational issues across the company.

Actions

Define the innovation "locations" and their needs: Consider the strategic scope and definition of innovation and the type of ideas that should be generated within your firm. Determine the appropriate organization to sponsor and support innovation within the many potential "locations" in your business. As we've recommended, a corporate innovation team or resource group is often good starting point. What will vary business to business are the "ownership" of the ideas and the staffing levels for the corporate innovation team, depending on the strengths of the lines of business and/or product groups and the need for focused innovation.

One significant challenge with a corporate innovation team is that innovation can become disconnected from the product teams that must implement the ideas and create new products or services. While a corporate innovation team can offer tools, training, techniques, and information, the idea sponsor and "owners" should remain part of the line of business or product group, so the idea, once evaluated and approved, can return to the teams where the ideas will be realized. If the corporate innovation team takes on too much of the idea creation and management, it may find that few product teams or lines of business will sponsor ideas because they did not create or evaluate them. The central innovation team should sponsor and encourage innovation in business units and product lines, and can "own" white space or disruptive innovation where the product lines and business units simply can't afford to spend time on ideas with long development cycles or higher risk profiles.

Define the appropriate structures for the type of innovation required and the organizational commitment: Innovation that happens in a single product group will require little change to the organizational structure. In fact, the team may operate much like a project team, forming to work on new ideas and convert those ideas into new products or services, and then disbanding once the development is complete. Innovation that spans product groups or business units will require more strategic management, due to the interaction of two or more teams with different cultures, organizational structures, metrics, and proposed outcomes. Innovation coordinated across a number of different locations may require the assistance of a central innovation team. Create a structure that makes sense according to the needs for innovation locally. This may mean that the innovation team is organized like a "venture team" within R&D, and other business units have an innovation advocate or consultant in place to act as a middleman for new ideas, which can then be sponsored locally or promoted to a central innovation team.

Define new roles in existing organizations: We've found great success in creating local innovation advocates or champions in each product group or line of business, similar to the Innovation Catalyst identified above. This person is a member of the product line or business unit who has received training in creativity and innovation methods and can act as an advocate or champion for innovation in his or her group. The advocate is a channel for information in two directions—communications from the innovation team and requests for assistance or promotion of ideas from his team to the corporate innovation team. Analogous to a Six Sigma black belt or green belt, the advocate plays an important role for innovation within his team and is recognized for the role he plays. Alternatively, the innovation advocate can belong to a central innovation team and provide coaching and innovation consulting to a number of different product groups and business functions.

There are three roles we advocate within a central innovation team that may be new to your organization. These roles are:

- Trend management and synthesis

- Process and data definition and management

- Innovation consultant/coach

The Trend management and synthesis role involves gathering trends, competitive information and market insights and synthesizing them in a manner that helps the organization understand what's likely to happen and how to take advantage of nascent trends. While some of this work is accomplished on a product line basis, it is rarely done at the corporate level in tune with the strategic intent of the business.

The Process and data management role is responsible for defining a consistent innovation process and data model and working to ensure that everyone in the firm working on innovation is following a similar process and is capturing and managing information using similar data structures to improve the firm's ability to "roll up" the innovation efforts and select or report on the work.

The innovation consultant role can take on a number of different responsibilities, including generating and evaluating "white space" ideas within the corporate team, or providing assistance to product teams or innovation teams within a business unit.

Establishing
measurements and
metrics

Background

Many organizations start from the premise that innovation is a worthwhile goal that will drive organic growth and marketing differentiation. What these firms fail to recognize is that ideas that can't be implemented or aren't valuable to a customer don't create any value. Too often, companies look at innovation with a "mom and apple pie" perspective—a sense that innovation is valuable in and of itself. While innovation can be valuable, that value is only realized once the ideas are implemented as new products, services, and business models. A common complaint about innovation is the difficulty in identifying the eventual benefits and results of an innovation initiative. Given the time period between the generation of an idea and its eventual market launch and success or failure in the marketplace, it can be difficult to measure the success of an innovation initiative. If innovation is to create products and services that create new revenue and profits, then innovation should be managed and measured as a process. Earlier in this book we've recommended that companies define an innovation process from ideation through new product or service launch. This "end to end" process should resemble other important end to end processes such as order to cash or procure to pay. Good processes can be measured based on their activities, throughput, and results. In this regard we recommend creating three types of metrics associated with your innovation initiative and process: participation, process-oriented metrics and outcome-based metrics. In the early phases of your innovation work, it will be hard to determine the "flow" of the ideas. Encouraging and measuring participation is most important. Once the process has become more effective and repeatable, you can turn to process-oriented metrics. Process-oriented metrics focus on the throughput and activities—how many ideas generated, how many ideas evaluated, average time from idea capture to launch, and so forth. These measurements can be compared to goals or expectations to determine if the innovation process is achieving its anticipated throughput. So, for example, we can set goals that our firm should generate 100 new ideas this quarter, resulting in the launch of 5 new products, and no idea should reside in the system for more than 100 days. The actual results of the process over that period can be gathered and assessed against the goals to determine if the processes are working effectively.

Many firms focused on innovation stop here. They capture a significant amount of data about throughput and congratulate themselves on measuring activities, but don't measure outcomes. However, we advocate a third set of metrics—outcome-based metrics that detail the impact of the idea over a reasonable period after launch. If the idea becomes a new product or service, did it achieve the market penetration and market share anticipated within the time frames as planned? Did the product increase revenue or profits or market share as expected? These outcome-based metrics are important because they form the "R" in ROI. Innovation, like any other significant investment or project, needs to demonstrate a return.

For a traditional business, the order of these metrics in terms of importance is reversed. Many businesses want to understand the return on an investment as the most important measure. However, where innovation is concerned, the return on any one idea will be quarters if not years in the future. Trying to measure an innovation initiative on these metrics too quickly will only result in the decision to end all innovation efforts since they don't create results very rapidly.

Case Study

One Fortune 500 manufacturing firm we worked with was struggling to demonstrate value from its innovation initiatives. There were a large number of ideas in the system, yet the team had little to show for its efforts over a twelve-month period. While some ideas had moved from initial capture to become new products, there was no method to capture the metrics around the process or establish the results for the new ideas as they entered the marketplace. Further, in some cases the ideas had never been evaluated to determine what the expected market impact and return should be. We worked with the firm to establish metrics and goals for the process. We also established a mini-business plan for each idea that was evaluated and moved into concept development or new product development, with associated timelines to judge the success or failure of the resulting product in the market after a reasonable period of time post-launch. This work helped the team gain credibility because they could demonstrate measurable value from innovation initiatives, and demonstrate how innovation delivered results tied to strategic goals.

Importance of Metrics

In our quantitative world, nothing gets funded that can't be measured and evaluated. We're told that most CEOs consider innovation a critical part of their corporate strategy. If innovation is a critical corporate process, it must be measured and managed like other processes. As noted above, innovation has three types of key metrics: participation, process metrics and results metrics.

Participation evaluates and measures the activity early in the development of an innovation process, before it makes sense to measure process goals. Process-oriented metrics set goals for the process itself. These metrics reflect the number of ideas captured, the number of ideas evaluated, and the number of ideas that become new products or services. Other metrics may include the average length of time an idea remains in the innovation process and how long it takes for an idea to move from initial capture into evaluation. These metrics reflect how well the process works and how active the ideas are within the process. It is important to establish and capture these metrics and report them regularly. This capture and reporting of activity metrics demonstrates the fact that the process is working consistently. Otherwise, innovation is likely to take on an episodic flavor—very active occasionally with large periods of inactivity. Since you may initially have few established processes and systems, your team may need to define and capture these metrics by hand as you develop the process. Some metrics that seem important early in the process will become less important over time as new metrics evolve. In the early stages of your innovation initiative, it is more important to communicate your goals and demonstrate results than to have the "perfect" set of metrics. These metrics are important for two reasons. First, they demonstrate that the process is "working" as designed. Ideas are flowing in, being evaluating and moved on to new product or service development or shelved. This "flow" of ideas is the only way to demonstrate that the innovation team and process is working until results are demonstrated once the ideas become new products or services and are launched in the marketplace. Second, they create benchmarks and indicate the importance and urgency of the initiative. If we create a process but don't establish measurements or metrics, then the message the executive teams sends is that the process is unimportant. Conversely, if the management team sets high goals for the process and proceeds to evaluate the results of that process, the message sent to the team and the organization is that the initiative is very important.

The "outcome metric" measures the success of an idea once it has been launched as a product or service. Based on its size and scope, an idea may return benefits immediately upon conversion or may require several quarters or years to establish a benefit. For each idea, establish a reasonable timeframe to demonstrate benefits and an expected return. Each idea should be evaluated against the metrics that are relevant for the idea and its benefits. An idea that improves customer satisfaction should be measured against customer satisfaction metrics over short time increments. Ideas that require deeper research and longer product development programs may be measured against revenue or profit goals over timeframes that span several years. These outcome-based metrics will demonstrate the return of the entire innovation initiative, in terms of increased customer satisfaction, improved marketing differentiation, or increased revenue or profits. The challenge inherent in these metrics is that many ideas will require investment in the short run and will not demonstrate a return for months or even years. In the early phases of your innovation initiative, be sure your team works on some ideas that can bear fruit quickly, and that you can demonstrate process-oriented metrics early in the process, since so many innovations may not provide significant benefits for quite some time.

Rewards and Recognition

We can't talk about measurements and metrics without talking about rewards and recognition. As these processes are new and somewhat risky, it is important to establish a clear set of rewards for people who are willing to start innovating. As the innovation work takes shape and your team can begin to measure the processes or outcomes, recognizing the people who are participating and their efforts and results will reinforce the importance that the management team places on innovation, which will have a direct bearing on the corporate culture.

Generally speaking, we emphasize intrinsic reward systems over extrinsic rewards. Placing too much emphasis on a monetary value for an idea is risky, as people will begin to hoard ideas just at a point when you are trying to encourage them to collaborate. Extrinsic rewards make sense not at idea generation, but once the ideas move into new product or service development, or proceed along key development milestones.

Intrinsic rewards have been proven in many innovative firms as the best approach. Intrinsic rewards, which may include recognition of the most active innovators, new titles, or the ability to participate in a new role as part of the innovation team, tend to have the most positive impact on the innovators and on the culture, and best support the goals of collaboration and innovation. As your team establishes its process metrics and outcome metrics and measures, consider how to best recognize the people who are participating.

Challenges without Metrics

Metrics create two problems. One problem is that metrics create an early, false sense of complacency. Management teams have been trained to manage and measure every activity, without always questioning the impact or results of the activity. Frequently the fact that we can report some activity seems to provide enough feedback that a program is working correctly. In fact it is difficult to determine early in an innovation process if the process is working well and at "optimum" efficiency. There will be a lot more qualitative evaluation of the process in the first 3 to 6 months than quantitative measurement. The other challenge with metrics is difficulty in defining the outcomes if metrics don't exist. Measurements, goals, and metrics are important, but early in this process the metrics can't be more than simple goals and measures of throughput—ideas generated, length of time from capture to evaluation, number of individuals participating, and so forth. Even in a very rapidly moving industry, product life cycles are 6 to 9 months, so moving from conception of the idea to a true market test of the idea can take over a year. And that's assuming an innovation process is already in place. Early on, it is important to establish some goals for the innovation process and begin capturing the actual metrics. Then, as the process matures, you'll want to reconsider the goals and metrics according to the results accomplished, and the key measurements and milestones necessary for the innovation process and for your company. The risk is that you'll be lulled into a false sense of comfort and security, because you are capturing measurements about idea throughput. In the early stages of your innovation initiative, this is important but somewhat irrelevant, because the real measure of success or failure from your innovation initiative will have to do with the market impact of the ideas you introduce.

It is important to set expectations with senior management very early on that you will not be able to quantify the benefits of the innovation work you are doing for at least 12 to 18 months. It will take that long to get an innovation process up and running, and move a few ideas down the funnel to become new products and services. If expectations about timeframe in which to see significant benefits are not set properly, the management team will seek to understand the benefits of innovation in one or two quarters—while you are still building out the team and process, and have not had the time to move a significant number of ideas through the pipeline. However, you must be able to track the market outcome of the ideas generated from the process, in order to demonstrate the benefits of innovation from new products and new services. These benefits may be come from a new product launch that generates new revenue, or a cost-cutting initiative that saves money and resources. Each idea that's converted into a new product or service generates some value, and you'll need to be able to point to those ideas as you report on the total value generated from the innovation initiative as new products and services in the marketplace to demonstrate the "R" of your ROI. The "I" will have been recorded a long time ago, and the senior executive team will want to know the return for the investment. Without the metrics and outcomes associated with the ideas you launch, you won't have the information necessary to justify the existence of the innovation team.

Actions

Define initial process and activity metrics for your ideas: Examine the types of ideas your team is likely to generate. Determine the measurements for the process (number of ideas in, number of ideas evaluated, etc) and the expected longer-term benefits for these ideas. These measurements and metrics should align with the types of ideas and with corporate goals. Define a reporting period, and report the established goals and actual results for the process.

Timeframe:	As soon as the innovation process is defined
Deliverable:	Document the types of acceptable measurements, timeframes and reporting requirements. Establish goals for the process and report on a regular basis.
Responsible:	Innovation lead and sponsor

Next, start measuring actual results of your stated objectives, once you believe the process is working well. Note the number of ideas generated, compared to the expected goal, and tweak expectations and behaviors if the actual results don't meet your early expectations. It is best to capture this information and act on it quickly and early in the process, in order to understand any undercurrents working against the innovation process. Understand that you may experience an early rush of ideas, as many people submit ideas they've been fostering for many years with no clear submission path. You may then experience a lull as many of the "low-hanging fruit" ideas have been taken out of play.

The goal for the innovation process is to eliminate this binge/purge phenomenon, but most firms experience this after first implementing the process.

Report results and compare actuals to expectations: As you capture ideas in your idea process, assign success metrics to each idea. What returns should the idea generate if it is successfully implemented? In what time period should those returns be recognized? These metrics can be set qualitatively or quantitatively, but for the process to work effectively you must set goals, and then measure the results. Once the ideas bear fruit as new products or services, close the loop and demonstrate the impact these ideas have on key success factors or performance indicators.

Timeframe:	Based on agreed reporting periods
Deliverable:	Identify the activity within the innovation program, idea throughput and compare to actuals for management team reporting
Responsible:	Innovation lead

Be careful not to place too much emphasis on the "wrong" metrics: Often, we'll see firms that have placed emphasis on the raw number of ideas that enter the system. While that metric is not necessarily wrong, it can place too much emphasis on volume over quality or broad participation. We prefer to see additional metrics, such as the number of people entering ideas in a given period, the anticipated impact of those ideas, and the potential uses or categories those ideas represent. Metrics are important, but must be balanced and aligned to the strategic intent of the innovation initiative. In a later chapter we'll review the concept of an innovation portfolio, which can be another indicator to help identify important measurements and metrics for ideas and provide the reporting necessary to make sense of your innovation pipeline.

Tie rewards and recognition to the achievement of agreed metrics: It's not enough to capture the metrics—you'll need to tie rewards and recognition to the achievement of the goals and milestones. These metrics may be at the level of individuals, teams, product groups, or lines of business. The constant consideration of the achievement of innovation milestones demonstrates the importance the management team places on innovation. Here you'll see why it was so important to set the correct expectations about the timeframes and return on investment earlier in the innovation initiative.

We advocate less emphasis on "rewards", especially monetary rewards for individuals, since we advocate a collaborative innovation process. Too much emphasis on rewards for individuals can lead to individuals hoarding ideas, unwilling to collaborate on ideas or share ideas if they risk losing the reward. If your innovation process is collaborative and if many people participate in the generation, management and evaluation of ideas, it will be hard to present a reward to one individual for any specific idea.

We advocate placing more emphasis on recognition—that is, identifying the people who are actively participating on ideas, submitting ideas and adding value to the innovation process. Especially early in the buildout of your innovation capability, you'll want to encourage and recognize participation. This recognition can take the form of a public ceremony for active innovators, to incorporating the most valuable and active innovators into your innovation team, or providing them with additional status in the same way that Six Sigma advocates become green belts or black belts.

More Reading/Resources:

Robert Shelton, in his excellent book *Making Innovation Work*, has a lot to say about innovation measurements and metrics.

DEFINING SYSTEMS AND DATABASES TO SUPPORT INNOVATION

Background

Right now, as you are reading this, someone, somewhere in your organization is capturing an idea. Whether they are writing it on a flipchart or whiteboard, or entering the idea in a Word document or Excel spreadsheet, ideas are being captured. That's the good news. The bad news is that it is very likely that there are a number of idea databases within your organization. None of those databases is visible to other users, and none of them can exchange or share data with other users quickly and easily. The databases, while valuable to the local teams, can't be easily consolidated and reported on to top management. Within your firm, as ideas are being captured, few people can find those ideas, work on those ideas, or add value to those ideas. While the concept of capturing ideas is great, the methods and tools most firms use are exceptionally poor. In an age where financial analysts use advanced statistical tools, and purchasing and manufacturing teams use enterprise-wide ERP and Supply Chain Management applications, the individuals working on the next best idea are doing so on the computer equivalent of the stone tablet. Think about this concept in terms of the purchasing process. When your firm creates a purchase order for goods or services, there's a standard process, form, and database to capture the purchase. Your firm has a standard approach to requisition, purchase, and receive goods, and a software application to capture and report that data. Everyone who creates a purchase order or purchases items uses the same software to capture their purchase requests and manage the purchasing process. We don't request that each team create their own purchasing software applications out of Excel or Word—that would be inefficient and difficult to manage. Yet that's the approach many firms take toward innovation—each group creates its own database of ideas and its own evaluation process. Why would we want every team to create their own ideation processes, forms, and databases?

Case Study

A major publisher we worked with had a number of different lines of business, each of which had an innovation initiative. Each line of business created its own idea database and captured ideas for new products and services. Some groups used Excel, some groups used Word, and some used Access or other simple database programs. These lines of business were locally optimized, but did not share innovation data across the enterprise. The executive team provided funding for some of the innovative ideas, but had no clear view of the ideas being worked and no "roll-up" or pipeline of the innovative ideas. As we began to review these idea databases, we found a wide variance across the groups as to what constituted an idea, what data was captured, and how it was captured. In a number of cases, we found that the same ideas were being worked on in different groups with no knowledge or recognition from their sister divisions. There was significant redundancy in the idea databases, and poor visibility of ideas across the enterprise. While the "local" idea databases were optimized for the product groups, they did not provide any value to the executive team or allow any collaboration with other groups. Simply by sharing the ideas across the enterprise, several ideas were combined and created a new business opportunity that none of the product groups could have accomplished alone.

Importance of the database

For innovation to become a repeatable, sustainable process, several components must exist. First, as we've discussed earlier, the organization must place a high value on innovation and break down any organizational or cultural barriers. Second, there must be a defined process or approach that people can understand, that is well-documented. We examined that issue earlier when we looked at defining an innovation process. Third, there needs to be a defined set of common, collaborative systems and databases to capture and manage the ideas, which works in conjunction with the defined processes. The collaborative systems and databases become important as an organization makes the conscious decision to become more innovative. As the number of ideas submitted, scrutiny of the ideas, and the number of participants in the innovation process all increase, a significant amount of information is generated and must be managed appropriately. While there may have been attempts to capture and manage ideas previously, few will support an innovation process effectively.

Historically, suggestion boxes and idea databases have been a disappointment. In the past, firms have periodically requested suggestions or ideas from their employees. Often, many ideas have been submitted, but few acted on and little feedback provided. Over a fairly short period of time, interest wanes as it becomes evident to the employees that their ideas are not taken seriously and are not implemented. From a management point of view, idea databases were ineffective because the ideas submitted were rarely focused on the strategy of the business and were either too tactical to matter or unaligned to the capabilities of the firm. So, large-scale suggestion boxes or idea databases have largely failed, not due to the inherent function of the database but due to the expectations and processes that surrounded the innovation initiative. These suggestion box approaches faced at least three significant hurdles. First, they are "reactive" in nature, allowing the submitter to dictate the idea and the context of the idea. In this regard the submitter enters ideas they believe are interesting or important. Often these ideas have little validity or alignment to the organization or its strategy. Second, the context of the ideas is difficult to understand or evaluate. Many times we've found great ideas in organizations that were poorly described or were not submitted "in context", so they were discarded. Third, there are few processes or methods for consideration or evaluation of the ideas that are entered. Even when ideas are aligned to the corporate strategy, there are no defined approaches or methods to consider and evaluate the ideas, so few are ever implemented. Since there is little communication and feedback about the ideas and their ultimate status, submitters lose interest when they don't receive any updates about their ideas.

What are the key requirements for an idea database? At a minimum a good idea database should:

- Be simple and intuitive to use

- Be broadly accessible

- Promote collaboration

- Be easily searchable

- Provide feedback to submitters to encourage more ideas

- Communicate the strategies of the firms and provide context about the types of ideas that are important

- Support and enable innovation processes

- Document the origin of the idea

- Capture statistics about the innovation process

- Provide visibility to ideas and the progress of those ideas to everyone involved in the innovation process

Also, an idea database should provide the innovation team with the framework to generate, capture, manage, and evaluate ideas.

A distributed, collaborative database removes the need for idea databases in Excel and Word documents scattered throughout your product teams and lines of business. As your firm moves to one standardized idea database, you'll experience several benefits:

- Consistent idea definitions. Rather than each team creating its own definition of an idea, a standard database will ensure ideas have some common "meta-data" and can be compared with greater ease.

- Collaboration. If all ideas are captured in one central database that everyone has access to, then ideas will receive more and broader scrutiny, leading to better evaluation of ideas earlier in the process and less redundancy.

- Visibility. The management team will have a much-improved understanding of the ideas that are being considered, and can more easily influence ideas that meet corporate goals and objectives, and better predict a pipeline of new products and services.

- A reduction of rework or redundancy. Ideas that have been considered previously can be identified before too much work is expended on them, and duplicative ideas can be merged to better apportion resources and personnel.

- Improved reporting and portfolio development. As the ideas reside in one consistent database, reporting the ideas that are in work and the breadth of the innovation portfolio will become much simpler.

Problems with the database

Too many firms expect that a system or database will solve their innovation challenges. In many instances, an innovation team will move to acquire and install an idea database before an innovation process is defined or the roles and responsibilities of the innovation team are created. As with any other enterprise application (for example, ERP, CRM or Supply Chain), an idea database or computer system automates and provides visibility and collaboration for data generated by the team or process. Where the process is inadequate or lacking, the idea database will not provide any benefit. A database will simply support and enable the people and processes that exist to generate, capture, and manage ideas—it cannot in and of itself create the cultural imperative to innovative or develop the process.

Without any database, an innovation team is limited to the number of ideas it can consider at any point in time, since there's no repository for ideas, and will face difficulty sharing those ideas or collaborating with other teams. In the case of local databases, each product group can generate and manage ideas locally, but there's little visibility or collaboration possible across groups. In the case of a centrally managed idea system, the impact on innovation will be noticed only as the database is part of a culture and a process supporting innovation. Otherwise the central repository becomes a database of ideas that is rarely updated or consulted and thus has little value to the organization.

Actions

Define your process and the types of ideas you'll capture before selecting a database: Define the types of ideas your team will capture and the innovation process you intend to follow. Define the evaluation criteria and the information your team needs to effectively evaluate and assess the value of an idea. Document these needs as requirements.

Evaluate commercial software using your defined requirements: There are a number of idea management applications available. Most of them are developed with a particular emphasis—idea management, intellectual property protection, idea generation, and so forth. While many of them have some overlapping capabilities, each also has a number of specific features and functions. It's important to evaluate several software applications and understand the perspective of the team that developed the applications, to ensure you choose a product can meet your needs.

Timeframe:	After the innovation process is defined
Deliverable:	Document the requirements of the idea management solution based on your team's goals and requirements in alignment with the defined innovation process
Responsible:	Innovation team

Consider building the software versus buying the software: In any enterprise software requirement, the team must make a judgment about building versus buying software. The benefits of building software are:

- The software will be built specifically to your firm's needs

- You can tailor the software directly to your requirements

- Your team controls the new features that are included over time

The challenges to building software in-house are:

• Developing the appropriate specifications to a detailed level

• Finding the right resources to develop the application

• Consistently adding new features and functions over time

• Development timeframes

Development timeframes are probably one of the biggest reasons why firms choose to purchase software rather than build it themselves. Commercial, off-the-shelf software can be installed and running in your environment in less than one month, while a custom development may take 6 to 12 months.

Determine your requirement for installing the software versus having it hosted. In some firms, the information technology requirements and security considerations will require that the software be installed in-house. However, in some firms, it may be permissible to evaluate a hosted software application that can be acquired on a licensed or subscription basis. In a hosted model, the vendor or another firm will host the software and your team will access the software over the web. Generally speaking, your team can start using hosted software within a day or two of your selection, since the software does not have to be installed in-house. However, there are occasional security concerns when a vendor or third party hosts the data. If you must install the software, plan for a 3-to 6-month window for your IT team to find the appropriate hardware, test the application, and deploy it within your environment. The timeframes will vary for each company but it will take a significant amount of time to install the software and have it ready to use within your business. You need to factor these timeframes into your project plans.

Incorporate your innovation process training and your software training as one training process if at all possible. Don't divorce the training for the innovation process from the training for the idea management software. Your goal should be to link the process and the software very tightly in your innovation community's thinking, and to use the software to reinforce the process.

Innovation software can have a significant impact on your innovation initiative. Just as ERP freed workers from managing transactions and allowed them to improve the management of the process and add value to the information, innovation software solutions can improve the effectiveness of your innovation initiative, cutting time and costs and improving the quality and outcomes of your ideas. However, if the system is not implemented in an environment where the processes, people, and culture are prepared, the systems will have the same acceptance rate as early CRM and ERP implementations, and innovation initiatives will fail even more quickly.

Maturity

Once your organization has defined its innovation process, acquired software to help manage the innovation process, and adapted the people within the organization and the culture to align with innovation initiatives, your innovation team can target other capabilities and attitudes that will move your firm into an even stronger innovation position. These capabilities and attitudes include:

- "Open" innovation—Receiving and managing ideas from individuals or organizations that are outside your business. Henry Chesbrough, who wrote the book entitled *Open Innovation*, has been especially influential on this topic.

- Creating an innovation portfolio. Some will argue that an innovation portfolio should be developed earlier in the development phases of your innovation capability. We think that too often the concept of a pipeline or portfolio of existing projects and ideas gets in the way of defining a new process and starting some ideas down the innovation flow. A portfolio is useful to offer your team insight into the areas where you have an abundance of ideas, and areas of your business that may be underserved from an innovation perspective. A portfolio view also helps ensure your innovation projects align with your firm's strategic goals.

- Innovation as an expectation. The final step in the maturation process turns everyone in the organization into an innovator. You'll move from expecting innovation from only a few people to sponsoring innovation broadly, to expecting everyone to generate great, useful ideas.

As your organization grows in experience and maturity, these capabilities take on new significance. Once you have achieved a measure of success with the first nine components, turn your attention to these last three.

OPENING UP TO IDEAS
FROM OTHER SOURCES

Background

The growth of the global economy has opened up the US market to many more products and services than were previously available, from a wide range of foreign competitors. The expansion of global markets has also opened new markets for US products and services overseas. The pace of change in the market is ever increasing, and new products and services can be delivered from a dizzying array of competitors. When markets were more protected and the global markets were not as competitive, innovation was less important as a strategic imperative, since competition was less fierce and change happened slowly. As global markets open up, competition increased from all corners of the globe. Many firms recognize that they need to increase the number of new product and service ideas, and that their internal capabilities aren't deep enough, or broad enough, to provide all the ideas they need. In addition, it is dangerous to assume that R&D centers in the US can predict what consumers in developing countries like India or Vietnam need as products and services. Perhaps the consumers and business partners in those countries, who are closer to the consumer than their needs, can shed more light on the product and service needs. As global markets open up, many firms realize that they must tap the collective knowledge of their customers, partners, and vendors to stay relevant and collect and evaluate the number and range of ideas they need. These concepts are not isolated only to small firms, or to firms with limited international exposure. Firms that have been considered the benchmarks of innovation—firms like Cargill, P&G and 3M—are opening up to ideas from a range of different sources as they recognize there are simply too many good ideas outside of their businesses to pass up.

Case Study

Proctor&Gamble, a firm many people would identify as very innovative, has recognized that there are simply too many firms and too many consumers in a global economy for all of its new product ideas to originate internally. If P&G tried to rely only on ideas from its R&D scientists and marketers, it would miss thousands of product opportunities that are available across the globe. Therefore, P&G set a goal: by 2009 over 50% of their products will originate from ideas submitted by business partners, competitors, or customers. This is a significant, audacious goal for open innovation from a recognized consumer products innovator, and it speaks to the number of opportunities and ideas that exist outside P&G.

While your firm does not have to adopt such an audacious goal, it should consider the sources of its ideas today, and determine the importance and relevance of ideas from partners, customers, and vendors. Few firms have a corner on the insight and intelligence necessary to lead a market for very long. Becoming more innovative internally is important, but identifying great ideas from inside and outside you organization is crucial for your long-term success. There are several approaches you may want to consider.

The first approach is **trend spotting and forecasting**. Examine what's happening in your market and with your customers and your prospects. Listening to your customers and watching the firms that aren't your customers will provide insights into the direction of the market. Identify trends and attempt to forecast them. What's likely to happen if a trend continues? What products or services will be important or necessary? Apple did this well with the iPod, not because it created another MP-3 player but because it brought a sense of style and a "whole product" solution to the MP-3 market through its iTunes store. Apple appears to be taking the same approach with the new iPhone. Your customers, partners, and vendors can help you define the trends in the industry and anticipate what's likely to happen in your market. It may be necessary to conduct qualitative research, or observational research such as ethnography, in order to fully explore the possibilities that may lead to ideas from these sources.

Another approach is **co-development** or partnering. Work with a business partner or customer to generate new ideas and bring those products to life. Leveraging the creative energy and capabilities of two firms with similar interests can create new categories of products and services, or provide insights that were missing previously. Often, partners will expose each other to new product opportunities or new markets that were not available previously, or create new product categories by combining the products or capabilities from the two firms.

A third approach is **open innovation**—allowing anyone, anywhere to submit ideas or suggest answers to specific challenges your firm faces. Certainly there are more ideas in the market than your firm can generate by itself—and customers and business partners want to have a stake in your products and services. Open innovation can be problematic, given that many of the ideas submitted will have uncertain provenance and legal standing. Determining the legal status of the idea and ensuring there are no legal issues inherent in pursuing the idea will slow down the acceptance of these ideas. Consulting firms like Venture2 are establishing open but proprietary networks of collaborators. These proprietary networks allow a single "anchor" customer to build networks of trusted partners that can understand and respond to needs for new ideas and technologies. This approach moves away from true "open" innovation, leveraging a number of partners in a network rather than a single partner in a co-development environment.

A fourth approach is a **published challenge**. Several firms exist today that will package your specific challenge and present the problem over the Internet to firms and organizations. Any registered firm can review the challenge and respond with a proposed solution. Probably one of the best known is Innocentive. While Innocentive is focused primarily on difficult scientific problems in chemistry and biology, the same approach can apply for your organization.

Another approach is to license or purchase technology or capabilities. In this regard, **business development** becomes an arm of the innovation initiative. There is a serious and ongoing debate about the ability of larger firms to create interesting, radical innovations within a conservative corporate culture. These firms may require a combination of internal innovation, open innovation and acquisition or partnering to provide a complete solution or portfolio of new products or technologies.

Clearly the first step to improving innovation is to define and manage your internal processes and capitalize on the great ideas within your organization. However, that effort only takes your organization part of the way to becoming a truly innovative organization. Opening up to ideas from any source helps your company identify and implement great ideas that will make your firm a leader.

Challenges with External Ideas

A firm just starting to improve its innovation capabilities probably does not have a big need for external or open innovation. After all, if you can't capture, record, and evaluate ideas from your own internal teams effectively, you won't have the processes and tools necessary to manage ideas from business partners, customers, and vendors, never mind the considerations of intellectual property. However, if you only rely on ideas from within your own organization and fail to tap the breadth of knowledge available outside your organization, you are relying on a very narrow perspective of the market and missing out on a lot of great information. Given the speed of change in the market and the breadth of the markets, most firms simply cannot absorb all of the available information and turn that information into new products and services quickly without relying on external partners. Without the insight that customers and vendors provide, firms may develop new products and services that are misaligned with the marketplace. When noted innovators like P&G and 3M focus so much of their innovation efforts on open innovation and working with customers and partners, clearly there is a large, untapped supply of ideas and innovations available, and a willing market as well.

If you choose to use ideas from external sources, you will encounter several issues or challenges. The most important issue you'll face is the question of ownership of the intellectual property. When ideas are submitted by a partner, vendor, customer or another interested party, your firm will need to establish the ownership of the idea and intellectual property, and also determine whether or not the idea infringes on any existing intellectual property. It can be very difficult to "prove" ownership of an idea, and the research can take a significant amount of time. While receiving ideas from a range of third parties can open up new opportunities, this process can also introduce a significantly higher amount of risk in your innovation process until the ownership and intellectual property rights of the idea have been established.

Actions

Determine your organizational ability to accept and use ideas from outside your organization. Review your strategic goals and directions. Is your firm prepared to gather ideas from external business partners, customers, and vendors, and create new products and services based on that input? Understand that tremendous expectations are created when you request new ideas from the external marketplace. You'll need to communicate effectively, and thoroughly describe the process and feedback mechanisms, in order to receive actionable and usable ideas.

Alert your business partners to your desire for new product and service ideas. One of the most important steps you can take once you decide to accept ideas from external partners is to publicize your willingness to work with them and to seek their input. Any partner who has worked with your firm has ideas about improvements in products, services, and business models. Communicate to your partners the areas that are most important to you and seek their input.

Define the process necessary to understand the legal issues associated with ideas submitted by third parties and business partners. Your team will need to devise a strategy to receive and review ideas and determine if there is any intellectual property concern with the ideas as submitted. Does the person who submitted the idea claim ownership? Does the idea infringe on any existing intellectual property? A thorough evaluation of the ideas submitted by your business partners and other third parties is definitely in your interest. To keep the review from slowing the process too much, prioritize the ideas that go through the evaluation and define key roadblocks or milestones to simplify the review.

More Reading/Resources

Henry Chesborough is considered the "father" of open innovation, and his book, entitled *Open Innovation* is a great source for further reading.

Mike Docherty, of Venture2, wrote a paper for the PDMA association that was recognized as one of the best articles for 2006. It is entitled A Primer on Open Innovation, and was published in the PDMA's Visions Magazine. You can find the article on Venture2's website: www.venture2.net.

A great new book by Barrett, Price and Hunt on intellectual property examines the changes in the management and protection of intellectual. *iProperty, Profiting from Ideas in an Age of Global Innovation* examines the generation, protection and management of intellectual property in a new light.

Building an Innovation
Portfolio

Background

New products and services don't exist in a vacuum—they compete with existing products and projects for funding and resources. As your innovation capability matures, your team will face an increasing need to balance the investments and focus of innovation with the existing ideas, products, and services already approved and under way within your company. Like any other investor, you'll need to create and review an investment portfolio for your innovation team. An innovation portfolio will help manage the ideas in process and help balance the number of ideas in a range of categories. An innovation portfolio is similar to an investment portfolio, helping your organization understand the value of the ideas, the areas where they are applicable, the impact they are likely to have on your market, and the risks associated with the ideas. In this manner your firm can determine if its idea portfolio is too heavily weighted to ideas that are incremental in nature, or if you have too many ideas that have a long gestation period.

As you begin your innovation process, you'll be able to implement the ideas as your team conceives them, but over time your innovation process will generate more ideas than your team can implement. You'll need a method to determine where your portfolio is weak and lacks enough ideas, and where your portfolio is relatively strong and does not require more ideas at that time. In this manner, the portfolio itself becomes an input into ideation and idea generation, indicating the areas of greatest concern or weakness in the portfolio. Likewise, a portfolio will indicate the distribution of the ideas across product groups or service offerings, and indicate which teams may need to generate more ideas to remain competitive in their industry. Finally, the portfolio will help your team understand how conservative or how risky the idea mix is at any point in time. For example, if the portfolio suggests your team has a preponderance of incremental ideas, and the management team expects more radical or disruptive innovation, your team will want to sponsor some innovation initiatives that gather more radical and disruptive ideas. The portfolio will indicate the risk profile, time frame, and value of the ideas that your team is considering and will expose areas of weakness in your innovation as well.

Case Study

A medical device manufacturer known for its innovation capability uses an innovation portfolio to help direct its innovation teams. The process begins with an examination of the existing innovation and product portfolio. The management team seeks balance between short-term, high-confidence ideas and long-term, risky, or disruptive ideas. Existing ideas are placed on an XY chart, where the Y axis is divided into old and new markets and the X axis is divided into old and new technologies. Ideas that rely on existing markets and technologies are in the "safest" quadrant—very low probability of failure, but also low returns. Ideas that introduce one new factor, either markets or technologies, are somewhat more risky, while ideas that introduce a new technology to a new market pose the greatest risk. These ideas are represented on the graph as circles with the size of the circle representing the potential revenue or profit. As a senior VP responsible for innovation remarked, "building an innovation portfolio requires tension between incremental ideas and disruptive ideas. A manager needs a scorecard or method to determine when these are in balance." Ideas within the portfolio must demonstrate three characteristics:

- They must be consistent with the strategic goals or vision of the company

- They must be achievable

- They must reflect market realities

As the VP noted, "there's schizophrenia in any innovation portfolio as a company tries to extend its hold on a particular market through incremental innovation, while examining the ways to disrupt the market through radical innovation."

Using the portfolio to manage the existing ideas and products helps the firm create balance between disruptive and incremental products and services and identifies gaps or areas for further investigation.

Importance of the portfolio

The portfolio becomes important as your innovation capability matures, since you'll create a pipeline or backlog of ideas. This is true because it's easier to generate ideas than it is to convert them to new products and services, and once an idea becomes a new product or service, it still must prove its value in the market. The portfolio helps to provide a map or framework for what ideas exist in different "spaces" within your business. For example, you may view your innovation portfolio based on the number of ideas that are incremental versus disruptive and find that a preponderance of the ideas in your portfolio are incremental rather than disruptive. This could be the desired state—or it could indicate that your team needs to spend more time generating and considering disruptive ideas.

The portfolio helps indicate where your team should spend its time—identifying gaps in the portfolio will help determine which ideas to consider or which product groups or business units need to spend more time focused on innovation. The portfolio should map closely to the strategic goals and objectives of the business as well. If the goal of the business is to create a significant number of disruptive ideas, then the portfolio should reflect a significant number of disruptive ideas.

Challenges with a Portfolio

Many firms don't use a product portfolio to their advantage, much less a portfolio that considers existing products and services and potential products and services. The first challenge is to simply create a portfolio that defines the existing offerings and identifies the competitive space based on corporate strategies. This means that the firm should determine its innovation strategies and document them, the assign the attributes or characteristics to existing products and ideas in order to report them effectively. Without a portfolio, it can be difficult to identify gaps in the product or service offering or areas where the firm has several competing offerings.

As the need for a portfolio becomes apparent, the challenge is to identify the appropriate reporting mechanisms and characteristics. Should the portfolio report ideas based on their risk, potential return, impact on the market (incremental/disruptive), cost or a host of other criteria. How does the portfolio reflect the corporate strategy and the balance between the need for current, short term revenue versus long term innovation?

Actions

Define the important strategic objectives and goals for your business or line of business: These objectives will help shape the categories used to classify the ideas and report the innovation pipeline. As ideas enter the pipeline and begin to mature and matriculate through the innovation process, they will be converted to new projects or products. These new solutions become part of the "portfolio" and dictate the ways in which the portfolio is measured and evaluated.

Define the best methods to report the portfolio to the management team. Many firms use an XY chart with X as the spectrum of technology change and Y as the spectrum of business solution, market or process change. The ideas are then placed on the XY chart as bubbles, with the size of the bubble reflecting the size or value of the idea in terms of dollars or market share. Other methods to report the portfolio may reflect the number of ideas that exist in the pipeline for specific business units or product groups, or the particular vertical or customer the idea is meant to target. What's important is the ability to present the existing product portfolio and ideas that are in process to the management team in a way that helps identify the investments the team is making and the balance of effort between new ideas and existing products.

Be careful not to swap ideas in and out constantly. While a firm can generate a number of great ideas, it is important to provide enough runway for the ideas you've selected as part of your portfolio to have a chance to prove themselves. If your management team is constantly reshuffling the ideas in the portfolio, this will discourage many innovators whose ideas did not receive the time they needed to come to fruition. The best advice is to establish clear milestones for each idea in the portfolio, and judge the ideas within the portfolio on their merits and their ability to achieve specific milestones—not to drop one idea already in the portfolio simply because an idea that appears "better" is presented.

Use the portfolio as an input to your ideation and idea generation. Once your innovation process is established and you've begun to collect a number of ideas and innovation projects, your team can use the portfolio as a method to determine the areas within your firm that need more focus than others. As your portfolio reports the distribution of ideas across the reporting topics, you may discover unintentional holes in the strategic coverage of the ideas you've generated. Using the portfolio, your innovation teams can direct their energies to important but underserved areas for ideation. While this is not usually the driver for an innovation portfolio, it can be the rationale that drives the most value.

Innovation as an
Expectation

Background

As your firm matures in its innovation quest, your company will move through several phases of innovation maturity. Initial innovation stages will include small innovation projects localized in product teams and in lines of business, meeting with occasional success and frequent failure. Over time, as the firm adopts more innovation techniques, innovation will become part of a business process, with goals and objectives and the requisite expectations. Finally, innovation will become part of the cultural expectation. Innovation will no longer be an "add-on" or a project, but will be part of the normal operating process. We can see this evolution reflected in the adoption of Six Sigma and other process improvement approaches. Today, after years of Six Sigma training, we expect any person who identifies a problem to identify it, report it, or fix it. This behavior has become ingrained in firms with a long-term focus on process improvement.

Over time, your firm should adopt the same behavior in regards to innovation. As your firm's innovation maturity level increases, innovation should become second nature. Everyone should understand the importance of innovation and how they can participate. Otherwise innovation is merely a "bolt-on" to your existing corporate structure and culture, and will lose focus when your quarterly results are disappointing. In this case innovation will never become a regular part of your business process.

Case Study

No book about innovation would be complete without a discussion of Google. Google represents a firm that expects all of its employees to innovate. Google has created a number of new offerings by leveraging a wide range of innovation approaches, including offering "20 percent time" to its employees. Twenty percent time is available to any employee who has an idea and wants to develop a new feature or product not currently planned. Now, this does not mean that everyone at Google receives every Friday to do whatever they want. Some people work on their ideas a few hours a day, and some receive dedicated time after completing a project. However, some of Google's best innovations were built by individuals on their own time or who were working on ideas or prototypes in the 20% time available to them.

According to Marissa Mayer, a VP at Google, over 50% of the product releases in 2005 were the result of people working on their own ideas or prototypes in their 20% time. Major new products such as Google News and Adsense were developed by individuals who had a strong interest in these applications which weren't part of the planned development process. Google encourages its employees to innovate and provides the room to do so. Note, however that simply generating ideas or building prototypes does not mean that the ideas will make it into the product, but Google taps an extraordinary amount of talent and interest by encouraging innovation from everyone in the organization.

Your firm may not have the ability to offer everyone 20% time, but it can place a significant emphasis on generating new ideas and eliminating the "not invented here" barrier many firms face to idea generation and new product development.

Importance of Expectation

So far in this document we've presented components that will help your innovation initiative get started and continue to gain credibility. Once your initiative is running effectively, the next significant step is to move beyond a "bolt-on" approach to incorporate innovation thinking and behavior as part of the standard corporate culture. Innovation must move from an "initiative" or project status to become part of the operating fabric of the organization. This change from initiative or bolt-on solution to cultural expectation happens gradually over time, as innovation becomes an internal expectation and minimum standard for doing business. This change happens through constant management reinforcement—

sticking with the approach when failures happen or when the quarterly results aren't the best. This change happens when people are trained to use the innovation tools and techniques that are available to them. This change happens when people are motivated and compensated to actively champion new ideas. In other words, this transition will take time and a lot of demonstration by the management team of the importance of innovation.

Challenges if innovation does not become an expectation

If innovation remains an afterthought or a process that is an overlay to existing business processes, then it will never become a functional process. When situations require more ideation and new ideas, the process will be leveraged, but the process will not be efficient since the process has not been consistently exercised. This will create frustration in the teams, since an investment in an innovation process has not made the capability more efficient. When the organization does not require innovation, few new ideas will enter the process and it will atrophy and become simply a database for ideas that will not be worked or evaluated. Eventually the team will lose faith in innovation and it will be noted as a failure in the organization.

Time Frames

As should be clear by now, creating a sustained innovation process and a culture of innovation within any business is not a short-term effort. This work requires real commitment and change over a significant time frame. If your goal is simply to generate some new ideas, that effort can be completed within a few weeks or months. If, on the other hand, your team expects to change the culture and expectations of the organization and create a sustainable, repeatable innovation process, the work will take much longer.

In most cases, you can expect to complete the first two components we identify (strategic alignment and management commitment) in relatively short order—often in as little as 30 to 60 days, depending on the commitment of the senior management team. What's key in the first two components is creating a strategic innovation charter that everyone can read and review, and obtaining management buy-in for the defined scope. In our experience, defining an innovation process can require another 30 to 60 days. This time will be spent considering how ideas should be generated, where they will "flow" and how they should be evaluated. As part of the process definition, you'll complete at least some of the work around defining roles and responsibilities, as the process will require definition of specific roles and tasks, and also dictate to some extent the requirements for an innovation database. Implementing the process can take another 60 to 90 days, as you begin to implement the plans and designed process. We recommend initiating some focused ideation or brainstorming in tandem with the implementation of the process, so you can quickly feed ideas into the process once you've defined and installed it.

It is possible to complete most of the first 5 components within 6 months if you have a dedicated innovation team, an engaged senior management team, and plenty of resources. This will mean that the process is in place and people understand their roles and responsibilities, and may mean that ideas are beginning to flow through the process. However, many firms should anticipate that completing the first five components will take at least 9 months, and possibly longer.

Once that work is done and ideas are beginning to flow through the process, your team will start capturing metrics, reshaping the organizational chart, and defining the databases necessary to support the innovation process. While all of that work is ongoing, your team must pay close attention to the needs for cultural change associated with your innovation work. These activities can span another 6 months or more.

So, it is entirely reasonable to expect that from a standing start, your organization won't have a sustainable innovation process for at least one year, and most likely the figure will be closer to 18 months, as all of the individuals, processes, and information necessary and budgets required to acquire the necessary supporting infrastructure will take more time and more effort than initially anticipated. Remember, in most cases you are:

- Creating an entirely new corporate process

- Building a new team from scratch

- Working with ideas, which are far less tangible than other transactional processes

- Defining new roles and responsibilities

- Changing the corporate culture and how people are measured and compensated

- While the business continues to operate effectively

These changes will take time to become embedded, so your team needs to set the right expectations up front. A good way to do this is to dissect the lifecycle of a successful product or service deployment in your organization. Most executives are familiar with the time it takes to develop a new idea as a product or service and then launch that new product or service into the market. When they speak of product lifecycles, they usually refer to this timeframe. However, in reality it usually takes at least as long to generate, capture and evaluate ideas which can be selected to enter the product or service development process as it does to develop and launch the new product or service.

In several firms where we've worked, we've partnered with the individuals in the innovation teams to unravel the total lifespan of successful products. In many cases we found that an idea was generated and spent several years in research and consideration before its acceptance into new product development. Then, the idea followed a traditional development path and eighteen to twenty four months later was launched as a new product. However, the end to end lifecycle from concept to launch for this idea wasn't eighteen to twenty four months—it was actually closer to five years. The management teams paid little attention to the lack of process and inefficiencies in the front end, and have optimized the development and launch phases. Only now are they becoming aware that a highly optimized development process is preceded by a fairly ineffective and inefficient innovation front end.

By identifying the total time and investment required to launch successful products, and emphasizing the importance of differentiation and speed to market, your team can place a much greater emphasis on investment in the innovation capabilities and inform the management team of the true lifecycle of an idea.

Here's an example of the true lifecycle of an idea. The Digital Light Processor (DLP) from Texas Instruments was developed by Dr. Larry Hornbeck in 1987 as a viable semiconductor technology. In 1993, the first LCD projectors and other prototypes were produced and in 1997 the first commercial projectors were sold with the DLP. At that time the management team considered the "lifecycle" of the DLP idea as about six years, from first manufacturing prototypes to first commercial product launch. In reality, the concept had been in development for close to 18 years, as Dr. Hornbeck and others had worked for years before developing a viable mirror-based technology.

Conclusion

Innovation is still a relatively new corporate focus. In many organizations an innovation leader is just taking on the responsibility to "make the firm more innovative". Few clear roadmaps exist to help direct an organization to become more "innovative". Hopefully we've demonstrated throughout this book that innovation is not the responsibility of one person, but of the entire enterprise, using tools and techniques that will seem familiar to most people within the organization. Unlike other business functions, innovation does not have a clearly defined organizational structure and crosses many key organizational boundaries. To implement innovation successfully, one must align innovation to strategic goals and slowly change the corporate culture and put in place a consistent innovation process.

How to get started

If you are just starting your innovation initiative, take the time to evaluate your company's position on each of the critical components we've identified. Work with a consulting partner or own your own to assess the readiness of each of these factors. Once your assessment is complete, select the components that need the most focus, and work on them to improve their capabilities. Once the important capabilities are in place and ready to work together effectively, turn on the innovation initiative.

Start small, with a focused pilot or specific group of innovators who are willing to work with you and your team to refine your innovation processes. Even though you've identified critical components for innovation, when your methods meet the real world of innovation, you will discover that refinements and changes are necessary. Evaluate the changes to ensure they add value and will provide consistent support across the organization, rather than allowing one team to set the innovation approach for the company. Once your team has completed a few innovation projects or pilots and refined your approach, open up the innovation process to a wider audience.

Broadening your reach

In any organization there are people who are more adept and more willing to take part in an innovation project than others. As you begin to open up your innovation approach to more teams and lines of business, identify the people who are most open to innovation, and create training for them to quickly distribute your innovation methods, processes, and language. Through this training and subsequent pilot projects within the new product teams or lines of business, you will create and begin to reinforce an innovation culture and a common set of processes.

Buying Time

Work with your management team to communicate that innovation is a long-term investment that can pay big dividends in the future. Identify some quick, small wins to illustrate the near-term potential, but also nurture some larger, disruptive innovations that pay off in the longer term. Keep your innovation teams tightly focused on concrete, measurable ideas that have attributes that contribute to one or more product team or corporate goals, so innovation clearly contributes to strategic goals.

Appendix A—Brainstorming/ Ideation Approach

Many firms have asked for a methodology to use to determine which idea generation and creativity tools are appropriate for specific situations. The best methodology we've seen for this selection is outlined in Stan Gryskiewicz's article for the Center for Creative Leadership called *Making Creativity Practical: Innovation that gets results*. In the article, Dr. Gryskiewicz examines a number of different idea generation techniques, including brainstorming, brain writing, problem restatement, excursion techniques and other approaches. The article describes a spectrum of scenarios that your firm is likely to experience and indicates which tools are most successful in the given scenarios. You can find Dr. Gryskiewicz's article at the Center for Creative Leadership's website—www.ccl.org.

We'll look briefly at one of the most common approaches to generating ideas. As you build your innovation processes, teams and culture, start working on ideas as soon as possible. Even though your team may not be complete, and the process may not be completely defined, the earlier you initiate some idea generation and start working those ideas, the more your team will learn about the process. Brainstorming is an important but overused and often misused approach to generating ideas, but probably one of the best approaches when working with a broad team that will not receive much training. We define brainstorming as a "real time" effort, usually confined to a face-to-face meeting where participants generate ideas for a very short time frame. You can also conduct an online brainstorm using software to record the ideas.

Brainstorming is appropriate when it is possible to gather a small set of people together who can represent a wide perspective and who meet for a short period of time to generate ideas around a specific topic. Brainstorming can be problematic if the individuals are easily influenced by a participant who is much more senior to the rest of the group, or if the dynamics of the group are dominated by one or two individuals. If these problems sound familiar, that's because they are some of the same problems that can occur in any type of meeting.

Brainstorming can be thought of as a specific type of meeting, and good meeting management concepts apply to brainstorms. For a brainstorm to operate effectively, it is important to have a defined agenda, a capable facilitator, and well-set, well-communicated expectations about outcomes. For brainstorming, we recommend creating a "framing" document which defines the opportunity, problem, or challenge that the team will use to generate ideas. Providing background, competitive analysis, trend information or other context about the brainstorm is helpful. A trained facilitator can keep the brainstorm moving effectively and balance the input across the participants. Setting expectations about the "next steps" is important, because too often a brainstorm is viewed as the end of a process, rather than just the first step in a process. Too often organizations will spend a significant time generating ideas in a brainstorm and fail to spend any time evaluating the ideas and determining potential next steps. This evaluation and decision-making part of the process must be kept separate from the brainstorming part of the process.

Every well-run meeting has an agenda, and every brainstorm we conduct, we has a "Framing Document". This document defines the opportunity, trend, threat, or challenge we seek to address in the brainstorm, and provides the importance of that issue and context. We define who will participate and our expected outcomes. We also provide any background material, market research, competitive intelligence or other information, so that everyone has a chance to read and review this information prior to the idea generation. In this manner we spend less time "coming up to speed" and more time on the same page and with the same intent. While it may seem a bit contradictory to provide this information and then ask people to brainstorm, we've found that by providing the scope and context of the opportunity or challenge the ideas generated are much more useful and can be considered and evaluated more easily.

Good facilitation is important in any meeting, and even more so in a brainstorm. Each brainstorm should have a designated facilitator who helps balance the discussion and input, makes sure everyone is on the same page, elicits responses from individuals who may be intimidated by the team and ensures all ideas receive consideration. A good ideation facilitator recognizes that all ideas are important, and that discussion or evaluation of the ideas too early in the process will choke off idea generation. He or she encourages the generation of a significant number of ideas—even those that are infeasible or impossible. The facilitator should be seen by the team as a person who is interested in their success but has no vested interest in the ideas.

Finally, the team must establish the concept that the work just begins as a brainstorm session or ideation ends. Ideas that are generated must be managed and evaluated.

Conducting an effective brainstorm

As we've noted above, an effective face to face brainstorm requires good preparation, placing the opportunity or challenge in context. It requires excellent facilitation, to ensure everyone participates and generates ideas effectively. A good brainstorm, however, also takes advantage of how our brains work. Often, trying to generate ideas in a very short time frame raises the sense of urgency and requires that ideas receive only a limited exploration. For this reason, we typically schedule a brainstorm over two consecutive days. In the first day, we'll establish the rationale for the brainstorm and conduct some brainstorming activities. Where possible, we'll work on activities related to the ideas that are generated, or on other trend watching, market research, or other activities. On the second day, we'll revisit the ideas that were generated the previous day and continue brainstorming. The rationale for this second pass at brainstorming is that very often the participants will generate ideas overnight as their subconscious mind considers the ideas more carefully and at greater depth. The concept of generating ideas in the shower is real—the mind works topically and at a much deeper level when allowed to. We recommend revisiting the ideas on the second day to reconsider the ideas that were generated and to capture the ideas that rise to the surface overnight. Finally, as part of the second day, we encourage our customers to begin to assign ideas to individuals or teams, for further consideration and next actions. In this manner, it is clear that the brainstorm is just the first step in the process of generating and evaluating ideas.

Brainstorming can be a powerful tool for generating ideas when it is used correctly. Managing a good brainstorm is much like managing a well-run meeting. Good facilitation, adequate preparation and the ability to suspend judgment while in the idea generation phase is important. One significant difference between brainstorming and a traditional meeting is the need for creativity. This can be inspired by allowing the team to draw, to encourage many people to speak and to consider very different perspectives.

About the Author

Throughout his career Jeffrey Phillips has been drawn to innovation—new methods, new technologies and new businesses. He has worked with a number of innovative companies, from large corporations in high technology fields like Texas Instruments, to venture funded startups and as a consultant. His interest in innovation led him to found OVO with several colleagues. Jeffrey is recognized as an innovation thought leader. He writes an ongoing blog about innovation (Innovate on Purpose) and speaks at innovation conferences. He works with OVO's clients to implement the methods and approaches detailed in this book to create sustainable, repeatable innovation.

About OVO

OVO is a consulting team helping our clients improve idea management and build sustainable innovation capabilities and processes. We help our clients generate, capture, manage and evaluate ideas to speed new product and service development and launch, driving increased revenue and profits. Through our Innovate on Purpose approach we help define innovation processes and align teams to corporate strategic goals. Additionally OVO builds software to create a collaborative framework for ideas and idea management. OVO is a division of NetCentrics.

For more information on OVO please see our website at www.OVOinnovation.com or call us at 919-844-5644 x789.

978-0-595-48425-6
0-595-48425-5

www.ingramcontent.com/pod-product-compliance
Lightning Source LLC
Chambersburg PA
CBHW030753180526
45163CB00003B/999